Don't Miss *the* Celebration *in* Heaven!

DON'T MISS
the
CELEBRATION
in
HEAVEN!

A Heart-Felt Plea to My
Roman Catholic Friends

PHILIP J. GENTLESK

XULON PRESS

Xulon Press
2301 Lucien Way #415
Maitland, FL 32751
407.339.4217
www.xulonpress.com

Unless otherwise noted, all scriptures quoted in this book are taken from
the New International version of the Holy Bible.® NIV®. Copyright © 1973,
1978, 1984 by International Bible Society®. Used by permission. All rights
reserved worldwide.

Printed in the United States of America.

Paperback ISBN-13: 978-1-66281-292-7
Hardcover ISBN-13: 978-1-66281-293-4
Ebook ISBN-13: 978-1-66281-294-1

DEDICATION

This book is dedicated with love, respect, and appreciation to my brother Dr. Mike, who the Lord made a great MD. God bless you, Mike, for helping thousands of people over so many years.

TABLE OF CONTENTS

CHAPTER ONE

HEAVEN IS WAITING FOR YOU

What no eye has seen, what no ear has heard, and what no human mind has conceived"— the things God has prepared for those who love him—these are the things God has revealed to us by his Spirit. — 1 Corinthians 2:9-10

In Psalm 37:25, King David writes, "I was young and now I am old." `I understand completely.

I was young – it seems like a short time ago – but I have now been breathing the air of this planet for more than 77 years. The years from 1943 to 2020 have shot by faster than I thought possible. In most ways, I still feel like I'm 35 years old, and when I look in the mirror, I'm surprised to see a grandfather staring back at me. I may not recall what I had for breakfast the day before yesterday, and yet things I said and did 30 or 40 years ago come back to me with crystal clarity.

At my age, I should probably be slowing down a bit, resting and taking it easy. But I can't do that, because a sense of urgency drives me

1

forward. I feel this urgency, first of all, because I know that no matter how many years I may have left, my life on earth will soon be over. I want to be completely prepared for the end of my life here, in order that I will be ready to start my new life in Heaven with Jesus. I also want to make sure that others are ready for the transition from this life to the next. I don't want anyone to miss out on the joys that await us all in Heaven!

Another reason for my sense of urgency is that everywhere I look, I see signs that Jesus' return is very near. He may come next month, next week, or even tomorrow. I want to do everything I can to make sure that everyone is ready for that amazing day.

Do you ever wonder what will happen to you after you die?

I don't.

Why not? Because I already know, beyond any doubt, that the moment after I take my final breath, I will cross into Heaven, where I will spend a joyful eternity in the presence of Jesus Christ and those He has redeemed through the sacrifice of His precious blood.

If you have accepted the forgiveness of sins that Jesus offers, then you don't need to have any doubts or fears about what will happen to you when your life on earth is through.

There is no reason to think that you might not qualify for Heaven, or that you'll have to go through years of cleansing punishment in a place called Purgatory. (Purgatory doesn't really exist, but I am getting ahead of myself.) The truth is that if you have accepted Jesus as your Lord and Savior you are Heaven-bound, no ifs ands or buts about it.

God does not play games with His children. If you are a Christian, you are simply waiting for the sanctification process to be completed. You have no reason to be anxious about your Heavenly status. As the Bible says:

> *"Do not be anxious about anything, but in everything, by prayer and petition, with thanksgiving, present your requests to God. And the peace of God, which transcends all understanding, will guard your hearts and your minds in Christ Jesus." (Philippians 4: 6-7)*

What does this verse mean when it tells us not to be anxious about anything? Precisely that. When we belong to God, we don't have to worry about *anything at all*. Even our own deaths. For the believer, there is no such thing as death. Rather, there is an immediate transition from this world to the next. One second you will be in this sinful broken world and the next you will be with Jesus in Paradise.

As the apostle Paul says in the eighth chapter of Romans:

> *"I am convinced that neither death nor life, neither angels nor demons, neither the present nor the future, nor any powers, neither height nor depth, nor anything else in all creation, will be able to separate us from the love of God that is in Christ Jesus our Lord." (Romans 8:38-39)*

Paul also writes, in the 15th chapter of 1st Corinthians:

> *"Death has been swallowed up in victory.'*
> *Where, O death, is your victory?*
> *Where, O death, is your sting?"*
> *The sting of death is sin, and the power of sin is the law. But*
> *thanks be to God! He gives us the victory through our Lord*
> *Jesus Christ. (Verses 54-57, NIV)*

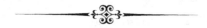

Sadly, many Christians struggle with the assurance of salvation. But please remember that your position in Jesus is safeguarded by the Holy Spirit. Eternal life is not something that you will possess someday. You receive eternal life the moment you surrender yourself to Jesus and He sends the Holy Spirit to live inside you.

Again, eternal life is a gift from God Almighty that He gives you once you have put your faith in Jesus. Nothing or no one can take that from you. Never doubt His word. Romans 8:1 tells us, "Therefore there is now no condemnation for those who are in Christ Jesus." God says you have eternal Life and that means you have it!

For the Christian, eternal life is not something you will have when you die. You have it now! You are already living it and it will continue after the hiccup in the road that we call death.

When Satan tries to accuse you by bringing up past sins, remind him of what the Bible says in Hebrews 8:12: *"For I will be merciful to their iniquities, And I will remember their sins no more."*

And in the Old Testament, Jeremiah 31:34 says, *"For I will forgive their iniquity, and their sin I will remember no more."*

When I was a young man, I knew a boy who was sure that he was going to Heaven when he died. The rest of us thought he was being presumptuous. How could anyone be sure of his salvation? I know now that he was right and the rest of us were wrong. God wants us to trust Him for everything we need, and that includes eternity in Heaven for all who know His Son and have accepted the forgiveness of sins He offers.

The only question, really, is whether you truly know Him and have surrendered your life to Him.

When I talk about knowing God, I'm not talking about an intellectual assent to His existence, but rather an intimate day-to-day relationship. There are many individuals who have read books, gone to seminary and conducted Bible studies, people who know the Bible front to back, can quote scriptures, and who attend church regularly, but who have not really invested in a relationship with God. Reading the Bible is one thing, but reading it to learn what to do in certain situations is quite different. God wants us to be totally dependent on Him. He wants us to continue to research the Bible to learn more about Jesus.

Jesus said, *"And this is life eternal, that they might know You the only true God, and Jesus Christ whom You have sent."* (John 17:3) And, *"You study the scriptures diligently because you think that in them you have eternal life. These are the very scriptures that testify about me, yet you refuse to come to me to have life."* (John 5:39-40)

Yes, death is inevitable. But those of us who are on a first-name basis with Jesus don't have to worry about it at all.

Everything and everyone dies! *Psalm 90:10 tells us, "The years of our life are seventy, or even by strength eighty; yet their span is but toil and trouble; they are soon gone, and we fly away."*

There you have it. The days of our lives are 70 years, or possibly 80 if we're strong. This is true no matter where you go, how physically fit you are, or how many organic greens you consume.

In Psalm 144:4 the Lord teaches us to number our days. What this means is that we should have a clear understanding that life here on earth is relatively short, that it will not go on forever. Death is coming, and we must be prepared for it. Many young people act as if they are immortal. They take all kinds of risks, without thinking that they are putting their lives in danger. But God wants us to live as if we will die tomorrow. No, I'm not talking about moping around and living in fear, but about making the moments count, about doing all the good we can as long as we have life in us, about storing up treasures in Heaven rather than grabbing all the riches we can while we're here in this world.

The Word of God tells us that humans are nothing more than "a mist that appears for a little while and then vanishes." (James 4:14) I'm old enough to know that this is true. Your life goes from child to adolescent to recently married to retiree with grandchildren in a flash.

Through it all you possess a sense of eternity. *The Bible says, "He has made everything beautiful in its time. He has also set eternity in the human heart, yet no man can fathom what God has done from beginning to end."* (Ecclesiastes 3:11)

In other words, God has put a 'You're not supposed to die button' in every human being. That is why we fight so hard to stay alive.

CHAPTER TWO

GROWING UP CATHOLIC

"Since my youth, God, you have taught me, and to this day I declare your marvelous deeds." Psalm 71:17

I don't know when life began for you, but for me it all started on June 15, 1943, when I was born into an Italian Catholic family. Life as a youngster was filled with love and traditions. I was blessed with many cousins, wonderful aunts and uncles, and of course loving grandparents who lived down the street and who worked very hard to prepare the 'family' for the difficulties and disappointments of this life. I never realized how quickly those days would pass.

Undoubtedly, you've heard many people say, "If only I could go back just one day to hug my mom and dad, to speak with my grandparents, or simply to share a holiday meal with the entire family." Nostalgia is understandable. We all miss "the good old days." But the Lord tells us, *"Let your eyes look straight ahead; fix your gaze directly before you."*

(Proverbs 4:25) The Lord wants us to focus on our eternal home, where we will see our loved ones again.

In my early years, I recall asking my mother if our neighbors, who were devout church-going Lutherans, would be in Heaven. Her reply was, "They are good, church-going people who love the Lord, so yes, I believe they will be in Heaven."

The Catholic Church of that day would have disagreed with what my mother said. I knew that, but I also liked our neighbors and so felt conflicted about it. It turns out Mom was correct, but I had to wait a few years, and a few Popes later to learn the truth. At that point in my life I seriously questioned why the Lord, as He was hanging on the cross, did not tell mankind to 'become Roman Catholic.' That, in my opinion, was very logical, and would have eliminated a lot of strife and cultural wars.

Although I am grateful to the Catholic Church for telling me about Jesus and instilling in me an understanding that there is one God in three Persons – I no longer consider myself to be a Roman Catholic. Why not? Frankly, because there are too many doctrines the Catholic Church teaches that are at odds with the truths found in the Word of God.

Again, let me say that I love much of what the Catholic Church stands for. And I love my Roman Catholic friends and neighbors. This book is not meant to be judgmental or critical. What I truly hope for is that everyone who reads it will ask God to reveal His truth. Christ

Himself said in John 8:31-32, *"If you hold to my teaching, you are really my disciples. Then you will know the Truth, and the Truth will set you free."*

What is the definition of 'Truth'?

The Merriam-Webster dictionary defines the truth as, "The real facts about something: the things that are true."

In the movie *Shooter*, which starred Mark Wahlberg, one of the characters is Senator Charles F. Meachum, played by actor Ned Beatty. Near the end of the movie, to demonstrate his continued arrogance, he says in a loud, dogmatic voice, "The truth is what I say it is." He is 100 percent wrong because he is a mortal man. If those words came out of the mouth of Christ, they would be 100 percent correct. In John 14:6 He says, *"I am the way and the truth and the life."* God doesn't give truth, He is Truth! At this point you may be wondering what this has to do with my Christian beliefs? Everything! Let me explain.

Growing up Catholic was easy. You simply went to Mass every Sunday and on Holy days and if you sinned you went to confession every Saturday afternoon. The Mass was celebrated in Latin, so I didn't understand a word of it, and neither did anybody else. Except, perhaps, for the high school Latin teacher.

If the purpose of Mass was to gain a deeper understanding of Christ and what He did for mankind on the cross, then it wasn't working. For most of us Catholics, what mattered most was following the rules, not developing a personal relationship with Jesus. Of course, God wants us to be obedient. The Bible is full of stories about people who succeeded greatly in life because they did what God told them to do: Noah, Abraham, Jacob, Joseph, Moses – and the list goes on and on. But more than anything else, God longs to have a personal relationship with His people.

Sometime in the 1970s, things began to change in the Roman Catholic Church. In many areas a new message was being preached — and in English! We learned what Protestants already knew —that we have a God who longs for a personal relationship with the people He created. Just as the Holy Spirit swept into Jerusalem in the form of a mighty wind on Pentecost Day, 2,000 years ago, the wind of the Spirit blew into the Roman Catholic Church around the world. During this time, many Catholics gave their lives to the Lord in small prayer groups. I was one of these and can recall that day like it happened yesterday. It was the day the Ayatollah Khomeini left France to return to Iran—February 1, 1979. I was sitting on my bed in Medford, New Jersey, reading. It was my wife Mary's habit of placing a Christian book on my nightstand in hopes that I would read it and say the sinner's prayer. Each time she placed a new book, I would check to see if it had an Imprimatur. I was what you might call a concrete Catholic. I prayed every night to 'the Virgin Mary' because I thought the Lord was out of reach. One day, my very patient wife placed a book by Albert H. Boudreau called *Born Again Catholic* on the nightstand, it had an Imprimatur, and was the book the Lord used to open my eyes.

Upon reaching page 153, I found the sinner's prayer. It basically directed me to admit I was a sinner, and said that like Jesus's mother Mary, we all need a Savior. As Romans 3:23 says, *"All have sinned and fall short of the glory of God."* In her Magnificat, Mary acknowledges her need for a Savior. Only sinners need a Savior. This was my first awakening. Mary was not conceived without sin as the church teaches. She was human, she was blessed, but not without sin.

I learned that I needed to accept Jesus as my Lord and Savior, acknowledging that He shed His blood to cleanse me from all my sins and unrighteousness. When I confessed my sins to Him, I felt such a sense of relief and forgiveness. I knew that my sins had been washed away and I received an unshakeable, unbreakable faith in who Jesus is and what He did for all mankind.

I understood that I couldn't ask anyone, including the Roman Catholic priest, to make me right with God. I had to accept Jesus for myself, asking Him to accept me into His kingdom and wash my sins away. The same is true of you. This is a very serious business, a transaction that can only happen between you and the One who gave His life for you.

The decision I made on that day over 40 years ago changed my life forever. Love and power surged into me as I stepped out of the darkness and into the kingdom of God. I felt alive in a way that I had never experienced before.

The next thing I had to do was let Christ take control of my life. Since then, I have repeated that prayer many times. You see, the old man of flesh that lives inside us has a hard time relinquishing control. God wants us to depend on Him in all situations, but the self doesn't want to let go. We must take up our cross daily (Luke 9:23). As Galatians 5:24 says, *"Those who belong to Christ Jesus have crucified the flesh with its passions and desires."*

The Lord, the God who created the universe, loves you and wants to be involved in every aspect of your life.

In Albert Boudreau's book, he states that he was determined to leave the church and give up Christianity after all his searches for God ended in failure. He recalls that his life was dull and powerless. Finally, in desperation, he cried out in prayer, "God if you are real, show me!" God responded and the author's dull, powerless life was transformed forever.[1]

You, too, can know the life-changing love and power of Jesus Christ.

This personal relationship with the living God is not something new. It's exactly what God wanted from the very beginning.

It is the heart of the Christian Walk.

Have you ever thought about why you chose to be a Catholic, a Baptist, a Lutheran, or a member of any other denomination? It's likely

---

[1] Boudreau, Albert H., "The Born-Again Catholic," (San Jose, Ca: Authors Choice Press) 2000

that you are a member of that particular denomination because you were born into it. In other words, you did not choose it. Your parents did. Or perhaps your grandparents.

For example, only about 2 percent of those who attend the Roman Catholic church in the United States are converts. And, you know, change is hard. It's easy to stay right where you've been, especially if you feel comfortable with the traditions and customs. Why step out of your comfort zone?

The answer is that the "comfort zone" may be lulling you to sleep. It may be keeping you from discovering the truth or having all the blessings God wants to give you. You may be like the frog, comfortable in a kettle of warm water, who doesn't realize that he is slowly being boiled to death.

The apostles and other first-century Jews who followed Jesus, made the difficult decision to leave their comfort zone behind. They made hard choices. A Jew who accepts Jesus as Savior and Messiah will most likely be thrown out of the synagogue. He loses an awful lot in order to accept Christ, but he realizes that what he has gained is worth much more than he lost. As the late missionary Jim Elliot said, "He is no fool who gives what he cannot keep to gain that which he cannot lose."

I believe we are all called to make the same difficult decisions. We cannot accept what has been handed down to us by our ancestors, but rather, must examine everything we have received to ensure that we are following the truth. As the Bible says about the Bereans, *"Now the Berean Jews were of more noble character than those in Thessalonica, for they received the message with great eagerness and examined the Scriptures every day to see if what Paul said was true."* (Acts 17:11)

As I've already said, it can be difficult to make the choice to leave behind something you have believed in and clung to since you were a child. But you will be given the grace you need to handle any circumstance that arise. I am not promising you an easy time of it down here on earth. What I am promising you is a glory-filled eternity. And this life is nothing when compared with eternity. We are more like May flies than we would like to acknowledge. Those insects may live only a few hours after first taking flight.

We lost our Golden Retriever several days ago. She was with us for 10 years, but it seems like such a short time. The Lord gave Mulligan to us when she was a pup and she became the best friend you could ever have. But she was only on loan to us, and the time quickly came for her to return to her Maker. Her death was terribly sad for my wife and me, but the Lord is carrying us through. We also know that the next 10 years will also go by in a blink.

And, while grieving over Mulligan, I received word of the passing of a dear friend from high school. I mention this to stress the idea of the brevity of life, and to remind us all about the importance of storing up treasures in Heaven, rather than on earth.

Our earthly treasures will not follow us to Heaven. The pharaohs of Egypt were buried with millions of dollars' worth of gold, many treasures and even soldiers to protect them. When these tombs were opened, hundreds of years later, all the treasures were intact, but the soldiers were nothing but dust. Therefore, store up everlasting and incorruptible treasures in Heaven. All our earthly possessions, idols like golf clubs, boats, cars, jewelry, etc. are useless in Heaven. In contrast, your heavenly treasures will count for all eternity. These ae treasures that you have amassed from serving the Lord, giving to the poor, tithing to your church, enduring persecution, loving your enemies, sharing the gospel, and performing other acts of service and obedience.

Because our life on this earth is so short, we have to make the most of it. We cannot spend our days trapped in false doctrine, believing half-truths about the nature of sin, salvation and the relationship between our Heavenly Father and the people He created. Frankly, I believe there are many areas where the Roman Catholic Church has mixed lies with truth, fables with biblical teaching, and spiritual realities with inventions from creative minds. The truth has been distorted to the point where it is barely recognizable.

Please understand that this book is not an attack on the Roman Catholic Church. But as someone who loves the Lord Jesus and His teachings, I feel that I must speak out when error is taught and people are trapped in spiritual confusion.

Perhaps the biggest difference between the Catholic and Protestant churches is that Catholics believe that the Bible is under subjection to the church's teachings, and Protestants, like me, believe that the church is subject to the Bible. The question is, who is the final authority on spiritual matters – the church or the Bible? And what do we do when what the church teaches is in direct opposition to what the Bible says?

I see no reason why any church should teach anything that contradicts the inspired Word of God. When that does happen, I believe we must accept the authority of the Bible.

Hebrews 12:4 says, *"For the word of God is alive and active. Sharper than any double-edged sword, it penetrates even to dividing soul and spirit, joints and marrow; it judges the thoughts and attitudes of the heart."*

And Paul wrote to young Timothy, *"But as for you, continue in what you have learned and have become convinced of, because you know those from whom you learned it, and how from infancy you have known the Holy Scriptures, which are able to make you wise for salvation through faith in Christ Jesus. All Scripture is God-breathed and is useful for teaching, rebuking, correcting and training in righteousness, so that the servant of God may be thoroughly equipped for every good work."* (2 Timothy 3:14-17.)

Another difference between Catholics and Protestants is that the Catholics have included a number of books in their Bible that Protestants do not accept as inspired. These books are collectively known as the Apocrypha.

According to well-known apologist Josh McDowell:

"These writings are not found in the Hebrew Old Testament, but they are contained in some manuscripts of the Septuagint, the Greek translation of the Hebrew Old Testament, which was completed around 250 B.C. in Alexandria, Egypt...

"'The case for including the Apocrypha as holy Scripture completely breaks down when examined. The New Testament writers may allude to the Apocrypha, but they *never* quote from it as holy Scripture or give the slightest hint that any of the books are inspired. If the Septuagint in the first century contained these books, which is by no means a proven fact, Jesus and His disciples completely ignored them...'"

McDowell goes on to say:

"There are some other telling reasons why the Apocrypha is rejected by the Protestant church. One of these deals with the unbiblical teaching of these questionable books, such as praying for the dead...

"Praying for the deceased, advocated in II Maccabees 12:45–46, is in direct opposition to Luke 16:25, 26 and Hebrews 9:27, among others. The Apocrypha also contains the episode which has God assisting Judith in a lie (Judith 9:10, 13).

"The Apocrypha contains demonstrable errors as well. Tobit was supposedly alive when Jeroboam staged his revolt in 931 B.C. and was still living at the time of the

Assyrian captivity (722 B.C.), yet the Book of Tobit says he lived only 158 years (Tobit 1:3-5; 14:11).

"Finally, there is no claim in any of these Apocryphal books as to divine inspiration. One need only read these works alongside the Bible to see the vast difference."[2]

John Ankerberg and John Weldon wrote a booklet titled *The Facts on Roman Catholicism*, in which they discuss this issue. "Perhaps the most serious issue in Catholicism is its unwillingness to accept biblical authority alone as the final determiner of Christian doctrine and practice. For example, by accepting Catholic tradition as a means of divine revelation, even biblically correct teachings in the Church became hedged about with unbiblical trimmings, which in turn tended to either revise, neutralize, or nullify these truths." Further "the problem is not so much a matter of denial of the truth, but rather such an addition to the truth that eventually it becomes a departure from it."[3]

Jesus actually addressed this issue when he told the Pharisees, "*You have let go of the commandments of God and are holding on to human traditions.*" (Mark 7:8) The New Living Translation Bible says it even better: "*For you ignore God's law and substitute your own tradition.*"

---

[2] Josh McDowell Ministries.com, "What is the Apocrypha? Why are these books not found in the Protestant Bible?" accessed November 22, 2020

[3] John Ankerberg, John Weldon, Dillon Burroughs, "The Facts on Roman Catholicism," (Eugene, Oregon; Harvest House Publishers) Copyright 1993 and 2009 by the John Ankerberg Theological Research Institute

You may be wondering when the traditions of men began to be given equal weight with the truths contained in the Scriptures? It actually began very early. Men passed information along by word of mouth, and it was written down over and over again. Errors slowly crept into what was written and those errors were then accepted as truth. It took literally hundreds of years for the teachings to be changed. It happened so slowly that nobody protested. In fact, most people didn't even recognize that the truth was being altered. In this way, the Roman Catholic Church was following the actions of the ancient Pharisees, who contributed their writings to a book called the Talmud. In the beginning the writings of the Talmud were viewed as commentaries on the Old Testament. But as time went by, the oral traditions that had been placed into the Talmud came to be considered as being on the same level with the teachings that are contained in the 39 canonical books of the Old Testament. Over time, the Jewish people were bound by hundreds of laws that controlled every aspect of their lives. Today, there are 613 laws (mitzvot) that faithful Orthodox Jews must follow. What did Jesus have to say about all this? Plenty! In the 23rd chapter of Matthew, He says:

> *"The teachers of the law and the Pharisees sit in Moses' seat. So you must be careful to do everything they tell you. But do not do what they do, for they do not practice what they preach. They tie up heavy, cumbersome loads and put them on other people's shoulders, but they themselves are not willing to lift a finger to move them...*

"Woe to you, teachers of the law and Pharisees, you hypocrites! You shut the door of the kingdom of Heaven in people's faces. You yourselves do not enter, nor will you let those enter who are trying to.

"Woe to you, teachers of the law and Pharisees, you hypocrites! You travel over land and sea to win a single convert, and when you have succeeded, you make them twice as much a child of hell as you are.

"Woe to you, blind guides! You say, 'If anyone swears by the temple, it means nothing; but anyone who swears by the gold of the temple is bound by that oath.' You blind fools! Which is greater: the gold, or the temple that makes the gold sacred? You also say, 'If anyone swears by the altar, it means nothing; but anyone who swears by the gift on the altar is bound by that oath.' You blind men! Which is greater: the gift, or the altar that makes the gift sacred? Therefore, anyone who swears by the altar swears by it and by everything on it. And anyone who swears by the temple swears by it and by the one who dwells in it. And anyone who swears by Heaven swears by God's throne and by the one who sits on it.

"Woe to you, teachers of the law and Pharisees, you hypocrites! You give a tenth of your spices—mint, dill and cumin. But you have neglected the more important matters of the law— justice, mercy and faithfulness. You should have practiced the latter, without neglecting the former. You blind guides! You strain out a gnat but swallow a camel.

"Woe to you, teachers of the law and Pharisees, you hypocrites! You clean the outside of the cup and dish, but inside they are full of greed and self-indulgence. Blind Pharisee! First clean the inside of the cup and dish, and then the outside also will be clean.

"Woe to you, teachers of the law and Pharisees, you hypocrites! You are like whitewashed tombs, which look beautiful on the outside but on the inside are full of the bones of the dead and everything unclean. In the same way, on the outside you appear to people as righteous but on the inside you are full of hypocrisy and wickedness."

Sadly, as we are about to see, in many ways the Roman Catholic church followed the example of the Scribes and Pharisees. In fact, in 1870, the Roman Catholic Church issued a decree saying that the Pope is infallible when it comes to spiritual matters. In other words, his pronouncements are on the same level with scripture. When I was a young man, I was told that it was a sin to eat meat on Friday. Why? Because Pope Peter said so, way back in 998 A.D., and that meant it was an absolute law. For nearly one thousand years, this was the case. Then in 1966, the law suddenly changed. Catholics are now allowed to eat meat on Friday, except during Lent. But Friday is still the day when most restaurants offer seafood specials, and clam chowder is often the soup du jour. The law has been overturned, but its impact lives on.

As you can see, if the Pope's pronouncements are law, over time scripture becomes relegated to the back of the bus. And eventually it fades away.

When I was an altar boy, I was told that "Scripture must be interpreted by a priest because lay people will not understand if they try to interpret it for themselves." This made no sense to me. Why would God put the Bible together in such a way that only priests could understand it? I especially wondered about this after reading the book of Hebrews, which says that once Christ came there was no longer a need for priests — and also 1 Timothy 2:4, which tells us that God "wants all people to be saved and to come to a knowledge of the truth."

Certainly, God wants every person to know the truth. He is not going to make His Word so hard for you to understand that only a priest can interpret it. That would run counter to His purposes.

Chapter Three

The Fundamentalist Catholic

I previously mentioned how the Lord used a book called *The Born-Again Catholic* to wake me up.

I loved that book and started sending out many copies to friends and relatives who, like me, had been born into devout Catholic families. I spent quite a bit of money doing that, and I probably should have asked the book's publisher for a job as a salesman! Unfortunately, most of my family members did not share my enthusiasm. More than a few of them thought I had gone over the edge, including my sister-in-law, Jurate.

She was a wonderful human being who became an attorney relatively late in life. She and my brother Mike, who is known to everyone in the family as Doctor Mike, were very busy people who still managed to do a great job raising seven children and getting all of them through college. My namesake nephew Philip went on to become an outstanding heart surgeon. It was he who sent me a book called *Born*

Fundamentalist, Born Again Catholic by David B. Currie.[4] More about that in just a moment.

My sister-in-law was, like me before Jesus changed my life, a concrete Catholic. She was from a European background, with very tight corridors. In other words, as far as she was concerned, there was no chance her beliefs could be wrong. On the other hand, she thought I had left the truth and got off on the wrong trail, and she didn't mind telling me all about it. I often tried to get back at her by asking, "When you die, who do you want to find waiting for you on the other side—the Pope or Jesus?"

Unfortunately, she passed away a few years ago, and never did answer my question. She, like most Catholics, loved the Lord and there was nothing about her Catholic convictions that would negate her belief in Jesus. After she died, I was thinking about her one day when the Lord brought to mind this verse from John 1:12: *"Yet to all who did receive him, to those who believed in his name, he gave the right to become children of God."* I was comforted by the realization that she was in Heaven with God. His grace is deeper and wider than most of us can ever understand. If there are any regrets in Heaven, I'm sure my sister-in-law regrets missing out on all the joy she could have experienced in this life if she'd had a personal, close, relationship with Jesus.

---

4 David B. Currie, "Born Fundamentalist Born Again Catholic," (San Francisco; St. Ignatius Press) 1996

Before we move on, I'd like to briefly touch on David Currie's book, *Born Fundamentalist, Born again Catholic.* The crux of his book relates to his upbringing by a fundamentalist preacher, and the fact that both his parents taught at Moody Bible Institute. He wrote his book to explain why he left Protestantism to become a Roman Catholic. Currie has a degree from Trinity International University and a masters from Trinity Evangelical Divinity School. He says he grew up believing that one became a Christian by acknowledging the fact that Christ died to pay the penalty for sin, admitting that your own efforts at Heaven were useless, and by accepting Christ as your personal Savior. This was the prerequisite of any "personal relationship" with God. His world revolved around the church. There was no smoking, no dancing, no swearing, or indulging in any other lascivious behavior. He believed that it was bad to be a liberal but far worse to be a Catholic. Currie cried over the death of President Kennedy, not because he was dead but because he knew he was going to hell!

Catholic beliefs and practices that Currie found offensive were the idol worship of Mary, the doctrine of Purgatory, prayers to saints, veneration of images, the daily crucifixion of Christ in the mass, etc. He says he felt lucky that he was not born Catholic.

How could someone who felt so strongly about the errors of Catholicism eventually become a practicing Catholic? Currie says the study of scripture changed his mind. "Just as the study of the Bible had earlier moved me from fundamentalism to evangelicalism, I now found it moving me *to Catholicism.*"[5]

He also says that "The Catholic Church views evangelicals as fellow Christians who agree with her on 80 percent of the issues." Personally, I would say that 80 percent is awfully high. Certainly, there are issues that most Catholics and Protestants would agree on. Both would agree that Jesus Christ is God incarnate, the only begotten Son of God who gave His life as payment for the sins of mankind. Further, we would agree that all humans are imperfect creatures who have been separated from God by our sins, and who stand in desperate need of grace.

But how do we obtain that grace? This is an important issue, because again, the Catholic Church teaches that it can be obtained only through the sacraments and teachings of the church.

Recently, I stumbled onto a radio program where a Catholic priest was taking call-in questions. Someone wanted to know if children who died went to Heaven.

The priest explained that of course they did—just as long as they had been baptized as infants. If they hadn't been baptized, they would go to a place called Limbo. (Limbo? There's another new place you won't read about in the Scriptures.) Limbo, apparently, is like Purgatory, except that it is not a place of punishment. But Limbo, apparently, is only for those children who died before they had reached the age where they know the difference between right and wrong. If a child should die after he or she was old enough to know right from wrong, but had

---

[5] Currie, "Born Fundamentalist Born Again Catholic"

not been baptized – well, then, according to that priest, he or she would wind up in hell. As you can see, there's not much room in his theology for grace. And his belief doesn't seem to line up with what Jesus said:

> *"At that time the disciples came to Jesus and asked, "Who, then, is the greatest in the kingdom of Heaven?"*
>
> *He called a little child to him, and placed the child among them. And he said: "Truly I tell you, unless you change and become like little children, you will never enter the kingdom of Heaven. Therefore, whoever takes the lowly position of this child is the greatest in the kingdom of Heaven. And whoever welcomes one such child in my name welcomes me."* *(Matthew 18:1-5)*

On another occasion, Jesus said, *"Let the little children come to me, and do not hinder them, for the kingdom of Heaven belongs to such as these."* (Matthew 19:14)

It seems to me that our Lord has a higher view of children than the Catholic radio show host.

Someone says, "But it's not fair to judge an entire church by one man's teaching."

True. But if the priest's views did not line up with those of the church, I doubt if he would be representing the church on a radio program.

Author Currie goes on to explain that one of the biggest reasons for his conversion was his study of a scripture that made no sense to him or other evangelicals. That scripture is Zechariah 14:20-21, which describes what it will be like in Jerusalem after the Lord's return:

"On that day...the cooking pots in the LORD's house will be like the sacred bowls in front of the altar. Every pot in Jerusalem and Judah will be holy to the LORD Almighty, and all who come to sacrifice will take some of the pots and cook in them."

Currie asks why this scripture talks of people coming to offer sacrifices if Jesus's sacrifice on the cross was all-sufficient? Will sacrifices continue after Jesus returns to establish His kingdom here on earth? Currie answers this question in the affirmative. He has come to believe that this verse is referring to a sacrifice that takes place daily in the Mass when the bread and wine are miraculously transformed into the literal body and blood of Jesus. But I have serious doubts about his explanation of this passage.

Read the rest of this chapter, and you will see that Zechariah is making it clear that God wants to make everything that was once profane (common) Holy instead. The bowls indicate additional atonement but not for sin. Everything within the city of Jerusalem will be made holy through the perfect work of Jesus. Zechariah ends his prophecy by stating very clearly that God will make everything Holy.

The first part of this chapter says, *"In that day there will be inscribed on the bells of the horses, 'Holy to The Lord.'"* Horses will not be used or needed for war any longer, but rather for godly purposes.

Despite Currie's contentions, this passage is not referring to the celebration of mass, or to anything (such as transubstantiation) that takes place during communion.

Currie also suggests that evangelicals miss the meaning of a Messianic prophecy found in the 110th Psalm, which says: *"The Lord has sworn and will not change His mind: You are a priest forever, in the order of Melchizedek."* (Psalm 110:4)

He says that by definition, a priest offers sacrifices, and points to Genesis 14:18, which tells us that Melchizedek brought bread and wine to Abraham. From this, Currie concludes that the Last Supper is the institution of a sacrifice. He tries to back up this point of view by quoting 1 Corinthians 11:24-25 which quotes Jesus at the Last Supper as saying, *"This is my body, which is broken for you; do this in remembrance of me."*

What Currie misses here is the fact that there are two priestly orders. The first is the order of Melchizedek. The Bible tells us that the Messiah has an Eternal Priesthood, after the order of Melchizedek. *(Hebrews 5:6, 5:10 and 6:20)]*

God revealed the second priestly order in Aaron, the brother of Moses. All of the Israelite priests were following in the footsteps of Aaron. Hebrews 7:17 emphasizes that Melchizedek's order is better than Aaron's because it is eternal and (7:21) says it is founded on a direct oath of God the Father.

Next, Currie gets to the crux of his new-found beliefs concerning the Eucharist. He says the very core of Catholicism is the belief in the real presence of Christ in the sacrifice of the Eucharist.

Currie says that he is 'bothered tremendously' by the fact that the God-fearing, by-the-book Jews passed down oral traditions from generation to generation. In other words, the Jews revered tradition as well as scripture. He further goes on to state that Jesus instructed the Jewish people to "obey the Pharisees." He is referring to Matthew 23:2-3, which says, "Then Jesus spoke to the crowds and to His disciples, saying, *"The scribes and the Pharisees have seated themselves in the chair of Moses; therefore all that they tell you, do and observe, but do not do according to their deeds; for they say things and do not do them."* Here, Jesus is warning the people not to get stuck in Pharisaic legalism. He wanted the people to have respect for the scribes and Pharisees because of the person they represented—Moses. But at the same time, he wanted them to be aware of the Pharisees' man-made laws and so-called traditions that had no basis in Judaism or in the writings of Moses.

Currie says that, "The seat of Moses was a product of that historic oral tradition so important to the Israelite faith. Jesus gives the authority of tradition his unqualified approval and commands his contemporaries to obey tradition's precepts." He goes on to say, "I have now come to the firm conclusion that the New Testament clearly and positively teaches (traditions) of the Church, just as we are under the obligation to obey mandates of the inspired New Testament. Disobedience of the one is just as serious as disobedience of the other." [6]

In order for us to understand this, it's important to get a clear idea of what "the chair of Moses" actually was. In every synagogue there was a seat provided for the rabbi. While he was reading from the law, the teacher would stand. When he was dissecting the meaning of what he had just read, he would sit on the chair provided him. That seat was the Chair of Moses.

It was not the teacher's job to be creating new traditions or coming up with new laws as he sat in that chair. It was, instead, his place to explain to his congregation what he had just read and let them know how they could apply God's Word to their daily lives. In other words, he had the same responsibility as befalls any Christian minister today. It is our pastors' duty to explain the Word of God to us in a way that we can understand it and use it to direct us in our daily life. After the service, the Jews gathered to discuss and debate what they had heard. They were not expected to accept everything the teacher said. If they felt he had deviated from the true meaning of the Scripture he was teaching, they let him know about it. They took their study of the Scriptures very seriously.

It would be a good thing if more Christians today were as zealous for the Word of God as the ancient Jews were.

---

[6] Currie, "Born Fundamentalist Born Again Catholic"

CHAPTER FOUR

WRONG TEACHINGS

The Catholic Church teaches that it can trace its origins all the way back to 32 A.D. Roman Catholic historians point to the Last Supper, just prior to Christ's crucifixion, when He breathed on his apostles and told them to receive the Holy Spirit. (John 20:22) They also refer to Acts 2:47 where the King James Version of the scriptures tell us that the Lord "added to the church daily such as were being saved." But was that the Roman Catholic Church they were being added to?

Not exactly.

The truth is that the Roman Catholic branch of the church did not come into existence until 300 years after Jesus rose from the dead, when Emperor Constantine issued his Edict of Milan.

Here are just a few of the questionable teachings that are accepted by the Roman Catholic Church:

The Apostle Peter was the First Pope

Did Jesus give Peter more authority than the other Apostles? The answer is "No!"

Christ gave the Apostles exactly the same power. The Apostles never recognized Peter as the Vicar of Christ. As a matter of fact James, the brother of John, took more of a leadership role in the early Church.

Peter never acted like he was in charge, never acted like a Pope. Yes, when Peter said that he and the other apostles knew that Jesus was the Messiah, the Son of God, Jesus said, "You are Peter, and upon this rock I will build my church." (Matthew 16:18) Jesus was not saying that Peter was the rock – even though He was making a pun about Peter's name, which is so close to the word "Petra," which means "rock."

The rock that the church would be built upon was the truth Peter had uttered, that Jesus is, indeed, the Son of God and Savior of the world.

In his book *The Humor of Christ*,[7] Elton Trueblood says that Jesus often used humor in his sermons and conversations with others. For example, His hearers probably laughed when they heard Him say that we need to get the log out of our own eye before we try to get the speck out of our brother's eye. Who can imagine someone walking around with a log in his eye? It's a hilarious picture. We often miss Christ's use of humor because we can't picture the Son of God smiling and laughing, like a regular person. And yet we know that He was a popular Man who was often invited to weddings, dinners and other festive gatherings.

Trueblood says that Jesus was being humorous when he made his remark about Peter's name and the rock-solid truth he had uttered. It was basically a pun. It was to affirm the truth Peter had uttered, and not a prophecy about his future. Peter was not the first Pope!

---

[7] Elton Trueblood, "The Humor of Christ," (New York; Harper & Row) 1964

Prayers for the Dead

There is nothing in the Bible that says the living should pray for the dead. When Jesus went to raise his friend Lazarus from the dead, He wept, but did not pray. (John 11:35) In the book of 2 Samuel, God punished David for his act of adultery with Bathsheba by bringing an illness on his infant son. As long as the child was alive, David prayed fervently for his healing. But when the baby died, David ceased his prayers. (2 Samuel 12:16-23)

Psalm 15:17, says, "*The dead do not praise the Lord, nor do any who go down into silence.*"

In my research for this book, I found that Paganism always makes room for prayers and offerings for the dead. In 1853, Scholar Alexander Hislop wrote in his book, *The Two Babylons*, "Thus Plato, speaking of the future judgment of the dead, holds out the hope of final deliverance for all, but maintains that, of "those who are judged...some must proceed to a subterranean place of judgment, where they shall sustain the punishment they have deserved." There is no mention of prayer to or for anyone dead, except the sacrifice known as the Telete. According to Plato, this mysterious sacrifice was offered for the living and the dead. It was taught that it would free a man from all the punishment he deserved for his wicked ways. This sacrifice caused people to spend large sums on funeral rites." Over 150 years since its publication, Hislop's book is still considered to be a valuable text on the origins of Catholicism, and has been reprinted by various publishers in recent years. I highly recommend it.

The Infallibility of the Pope

According to the Roman Catholic Church, the Pope is preserved from the possibility of error when he speaks from the chair of St. Peter's Basilica (ex cathedra), on matters of faith and morals. What this means is that whatever he says in an official capacity then beomes a doctrine of the church. This infallibility does not carry over to all announcements from the Pope. The last time the Pope spoke ex cathedra was over 70 years ago, in 1950. That was when Pope Pius XII announced that Mary's assumption into Heaven, without experiencing death, was now official church doctrine. From that date forward, if you wanted to be a faithful Catholic, you had to believe this was true.

Obviously, I do not accept the teaching that the Pope is infallible in any way. There have been too many Popes whose lives did not line up with this belief. Popes who have had children, a Pope who sided with Hitler and Mussolini, and Popes who were more interested in making money than in helping the poor. And Popes who made contradictory decisions.

Pope (Eugene IV (1431/47) put Joan of Arc to death, while Benedict (1919) made her a saint.

Gregory I (590-604) made it clear that anyone who took the title of Universal Bishop was an antichrist; but Boniface III (607) demanded that the emperor Phocas offer that title to him. And it has been used by all Popes since.

Interestingly there are no scriptures to support this infallibility issue. What you do find are several powerful dissenters. One in particular was

Archbishop Strossmayer, who boldly stated that he rejected the idea of an 'infallible Pope.'[8]

The Veneration of Mary

The announcement that Mary's assumption into Heaven had become official church doctrine was just one more step in the church's elevation of Mary. Over the centuries, the Catholic Church has increased her importance to the point where she has almost become a member of the Trinity. The way the church venerates and exalts Mary reminds me that many ancient Jews worshiped the Queen of Heaven, whom they considered to be God's wife.

Speaking through the Prophet Jeremiah, God said, *"Do you not see what they are doing in the towns of Judah and in the streets of Jerusalem? The children gather wood, the fathers light the fire, and the women knead the dough and make cakes to offer to the Queen of Heaven. They pour out drink offerings to other gods to arouse my anger. But am I the one they are provoking? declares the* LORD. *Are they not rather harming themselves, to their own shame?" (Jeremiah 7:17-19)*

Certainly, Mary deserves to be honored. God chose her to give birth to His Son. What an absolutely amazing blessing! And yet, the book of Luke records this incident:

"Now Jesus' mother and brothers came to see him, but they were not able to get near him because of the crowd. Someone

---

[8] The Catholic Encyclopedia (©1913 Vol. XIV p.316)

told him, 'Your mother and brothers are standing outside, wanting to see you.'

"He replied, 'My mother and brothers are those who hear God's word and put it into practice.'" (Luke 8:20-21)

On another occasion, a woman called out to Jesus, "Blessed is the mother who gave you birth and nursed you." He replied, *"Blessed rather are those who hear the word of God and obey it."* (Luke 11:27)

Jesus certainly loved His mother. One of His last acts, as He hung on the cross, was to ask the apostle John to take her into his home and care for her. But He never suggested that she should be treated as if she were divine.

Another thing the Roman Catholic Church has done, which to my understanding does not coincide with reality, is to honor Mary as an eternal virgin. Take another look at the passage from the eighth chapter of Luke, and you'll see that Jesus was told that his mother and brothers were outside waiting for Him. But how was it possible for Jesus to have brothers if His mother was still a virgin? Ask your local priest and he will tell you that these were not Jesus's brothers, but rather His cousins. And yet, Paul wrote about Mark, the cousin of Barnabas. (Colossians 4:10) And John the Baptist, who was Jesus's cousin, is never referred to as His brother. The men who wrote the Bible knew the difference between brothers and cousins, and there was no reason for them to confuse the two. In fact, Matthew 1:25 says that Joseph and Mary did not consummate their marriage until after Jesus was born. The Bible does not say that they never consummated their marriage. She was not a perpetual virgin.

In addition to that, when Jesus taught in His hometown synagogue, some of those present mentioned his brothers by name:

> *"Coming to his hometown, he began teaching the people in their synagogue, and they were amazed. 'Where did this man get this wisdom and these miraculous powers?' they asked. 'Isn't this the carpenter's son? Isn't his mother's name Mary, and aren't his brothers James, Joseph, Simon and Judas? Aren't all his sisters with us? Where then did this man get all these things?' And they took offense at him."* (Matthew 13-54-57)

In light of these passages, how can the Catholic Church say that Mary was a virgin her entire life? I realize that it doesn't really matter whether or not Mary was a virgin. What you believe about this does not affect your salvation in any way. But this is just one of many times where Catholic tradition does not square up with what the Bible says.

Penance:

The Bible says that we are saved by grace, yet the Catholic Church would have us believe that we can't be saved unless we confess our sins to a priest. According to the Baltimore Catechism, the sins that we commit after our baptism can be forgiven only through the absolution of a priest. The reason why I have a major problem with this is that the Bible tells us in 1 John 1:9, *"Confess your sins to God."*

The concept of confessing to a priest is not found in the Bible. In fact, in 1 Peter 2:5-9, we are told that believers are a holy priesthood, and again in Revelation 1:6, we are called a royal priesthood. **God sees us as a kingdom of priests.**

Clearly, priests were an important part of the Jewish religion. The priests were the only ones who could offer sacrifices on behalf of the people. Only the priests were allowed to go beyond the curtain into the Holy of Holies, directly into the presence of God. But when Jesus died on the cross, the Bible tell us that the curtain was torn in two, from the top to the bottom. (Matthew 27:51) This meant that from now on, God's people were allowed to go directly into His presence.

From that time forward, there has no longer been any need for a priest to serve as a go-between us and God. Jesus is our high priest, and we have no need for any other. And, by the way, it is significant that the curtain was rent from top to bottom. It was God who tore the temple, welcoming us directly into His presence.

Because of what Jesus did for us, the Bible says, *"Let us then with confidence draw near to the throne of Grace, that we may receive mercy and find grace to help in time of need."* (Hebrews 4:16)

Hebrews also tells us, *"Therefore, brothers, since we have confidence to enter the holy places by the blood of Jesus, by the New and Living way that He opened for us through the curtain, that is through the flesh, and since we have a great priest over the house of God, let us draw near with a true heart in full assurance of faith, with our hearts sprinkled clean from an evil conscience and our bodies washed with pure water."* (Hebrews 4:16)

According to Catholicism, our salvation depends on what we do (works) rather than on God's love and mercy. But the Bible tells us, *"For it is by grace you have been saved, through faith, and this not from yourselves, it is the gift of God – not by works so that no one can boast."* (Ephesians 2:8-9)

When you accept Christ and are born again, you are forgiven. God now begins the process of sanctification. All you need to do is to allow the Holy Spirit to prepare you for your Heavenly home. You will find that you no longer want to do the worldly things that lead away from God. The appetite for sin and worldly things will be stripped away as the love of God transforms you.

You may lose some friends along the way, but you will make new ones who believe as you do. You may be ridiculed and laughed at in certain settings, but eventually the same people who ridicule you now, will want what you have. The Lord loves them and He wants everyone to be saved.

In Loraine Boettner's book, Roman Catholicism, he says "We searched in vain in the Bible for any word supporting the doctrine of 'auricular confession,' no evidence to support it in the first thousand years of the church. Not even a word in any of the early church father's writings. Not found in writings of Augustine, Origen, Nestorius, Tertullian, Jerome, and so on. None! Most of their writings were concerned with

Christian living. Not one of the above even on their death bed, thought of confession to a priest. Confession was first introduced as "voluntary" in the fifth century. Made mandatory in 1215 by the Pope."[9]

The biggest problem for the priests at that time was to reach an agreement on which sins were venial and which were morltal. The Pope never actually made an announcement regarding which sins were which. That was pretty much left up to the interpretation of the parish priests, so ordinary Catholics were left guessing whether or not they had actually been forgiven.

Prayers to the Saints

As we just discussed, when Jesus died, the curtain in the temple was torn in two, allowing ordinary humans like you and me to come directly into God's presence. From that moment on, there has been no need for priests to serve as intermediaries between God and man.

Unfortunately, over the centuries, the Roman Catholic Church has increased the space between Christ and His people by giving us an ever-increasing list of saints to pray to. I have already mentioned how I once prayed to the Virgin Mary every night because I believed Christ was too high and distant to pay attention to me. I know I wasn't the only Catholic to feel that way. Instead of helping us draw nearer to Jesus, as He desires, the Catholic Church has set up a long chain of "saints" to keep us at a distance. The truth is that Jesus loves us all more

---

[9] Lorraine Boettner, "Roman Catholicism," (Grand Rapids, MI: Baker Books) 1983

than we can possibly know, and He wants us to come directly to Him. He calls out to us:

> *"Come to me, all you who are weary and burdened, and I will give you rest. Take my yoke up you and learn from me, for I am gentle and humble in heart, and you will find rest for your souls. For my yoke is easy and my burden is light."* Matthew 11 28:30)

How does He listen to the prayers of billions of people at once? I don't know, but that's because I am a finite human being with a very limited understanding of spiritual reality, and He is God! I believe that He cares for you as if you were the only person in the world.

I understand that Jesus came into this world to give His life for us so that we can be reconciled with God and spend eternity in Heaven. But I also believe he came to experience life as a human being so that He could have a complete understanding of what life is like for us. As the writer of Hebrews says:

> *"For we do not have a high priest who is unable to sympathize with our weaknesses, but we have one who has been tempted in every way, just as we are—yet without sin. Let us them approach the throne of grace with confidence, so that we may receive mercy and find grace to help us in our time of need."* (Hebrews 4:15-16)

Jesus knows what it's like to have a stomach that aches from hunger. As a young man, working in Joseph's carpenter shop, he undoubtedly experienced smashed fingers and cuts that wouldn't stop bleeding. He knows the pain of a throbbing headache, and the sorrow of bereavement. Whatever you've gone through, Jesus has been there, too. He knows how you feel, and that makes Him the perfect "high priest." We don't need to turn to a saint who is supposed to protect people when they travel, or another who helps us find important items we've lost. We can and should turn to Jesus Himself with all our requests and our praise.

And by the way, if you are someone who has accepted Jesus Christ as your Lord and Savior, you may be surprised to learn that you are a saint. You don't have to wait to be beatified by the Pope and the College of Cardinals.

In Paul's epistles he often used the word, "saints" to refer to the individual members of churches. For instance, he urges members of the church at Ephesus to "keep on praying for all the saints." (Ephesians 6:18) If you are not a saint, you can become one today. It's easy. All you have to do is accept Jesus Christ as your Lord and Savior. If you haven't already done this, why not do it right now? Just tell Him in your own words that you believe He is the Son of God who died for you, was buried, and rose again on the third day. Ask Him to forgive your sins, to take his rightful place as your Lord and Savior and tell Him you want to serve Him the rest of your life. That simple prayer will take you out of the darkness and into the eternal light of His kingdom.

I would write out a prayer for you to follow, and you can find many different versions of "the sinner's prayer" in books and online. But I don't want you to view this prayer as a part of some liturgy. I urge you to say it in your own words, using feelings that come directly from your heart. It doesn't matter if the words don't come out exactly as you want them to, or if you stumble around a bit. God knows what is in your heart and He hears your words in that context. Romans 8:26 says, "And the Holy Spirit helps us in our weakness. For example, we don't know what God wants us to pray for. But the Holy Spirit prays for us with groanings that cannot be expressed in words." (NLT)

Now, before moving on, I do want to say a few words about something that many people could learn from the Catholic Church – and that is a reverence for the Person of Jesus Christ. I believe they are wrong to present our loving and compassionate Savior as someone who is too sacred and holy to be approached by ordinary men and women like you and me. But I do appreciate the reverence they show for Him. I would love to see Christians of all denominations—Baptists, Lutherans, Methodists, Charismatics, and so on—spend more time on their knees before the Lord. It makes me happy that over the past 20 years or so, many churches have begun spending more and more time in praise and worship. Yes, Jesus is our friend. He promises that wherever two or three are gathered in His name, there is He in the midst of them. There are no walls between us. But we must understand that He is not our best buddy – the guy next door. He is God and should be revered and worshiped as such.

The Mass and Transubstantiation

The Roman Catholic catechism states that Christ initiated the Mass at last supper, and basically gave it to man as a lasting remembrance. It further states that the Mass is the same sacrifice as the sacrifice on the cross. In other words, each time you attend Mass and partake of communion, it is as if you are being saved all over again.

The Old Testament teaches that when the Jewish priests offered a sacrifice for the people, their sins were not forgiven, but rather rolled forward until the time of the next sacrifice. This would continue until the perfect sacrifice was offered that would erase the people's sins for all time. As we know, that perfect sacrifice came when Jesus was offered up on a hill called Golgotha. After this, there was no longer any need to push sins forward until the next sacrifice was offered. But, in essence, the Roman Catholic church still teaches that your sins are moved forward until your next Communion, your next Mass, your next time of Confession. You are forgiven bit by bit, but can never have the satisfaction of knowing that you have been declared blameless through the blood of Christ.

Now, Catholic theology tells us that, through a miraculous process called transubstantiation, the bread and wine that are used in communion are transformed into the actual body and blood of Jesus Christ. This is a literal translation of the passage found in the 26th chapter of Matthew:

"While they were eating, Jesus took bread, gave thanks and broke it, and gave it to his disciples, saying, 'Take and eat, this is my body.'

"Then he took the cup, gave thanks and offered it to them, saying, 'Drink from it, all of you. This is my blood of the covenant, which is poured out for man for the forgiveness of sins.'"

In the 11ᵗʰ chapter of 1 Corinthians, Paul writes:

"For I received from the Lord what I also passed on to you. The Lord Jesus, on the night he was betrayed took bread, and when he had given thanks he broke it and said, 'This is my body, which is for you; do this in remembrance. Of me.' In the same way after supper he took the cup saying, 'This cup is the new covenant in my blood; do this, whenever you drink it, in remembrance of me. For whenever you eat this bread and drink this cup, you proclaim the Lord's death until he comes." (1 Corinthians 11:23-26)

It should be clear from this passage that the wine and the bread that are served in communion are symbolic of how Jesus's body was broken and His blood shed. I believe there is power in the bread and wine because it connects us to Christ in a way that is too wonderful for us to understand. But if it were the actual blood and body of Jesus, then I am quite sure He would have told us so, and Paul would have corroborated that fact.

In fact, the Bible tells us, in Hebrews 7:27, that, "Unlike the other high priests, he (Christ) does not need to offer sacrifices day after day, first for his own sins, and then for the sins of the people. He sacrificed for their sins once for all when he offered himself." Again, in Hebrews 9:12, we read, "He did not enter by means of the blood of goats and calves; but he entered the Most Holy Place once for all by his own blood, thus obtaining eternal redemption."

Other scriptures say the same thing. Christ died once as an atonement for the sins of all men and women, and there is no need for a further sacrifice.

If you are a Roman Catholic, the importance of Mass and communion have been drilled into your brain your entire life. You were taught that you cannot be saved without your involvement in these Sacraments of the church, but this is simply not true. You are saved through faith in Jesus and His sacrifice for you on a long-ago Friday. The only thing you have to do is accept the gift of eternal life He gives.

You may be wondering when the Church first began teaching that attendance at Mass is an essential component for salvation.

It was first proposed by Paschasius Radbertus a Benedictine monk who lived in the ninth century, but it was not until 1215 at the Lateran Council that attendance at Mass was officially designated as mandatory.

Now, of course, the Fourth of the Ten Commandments is, "Remember the Sabbath Day by keeping it holy." (Exodus 20:8)

As I've mentioned previously, I grew up very Catholic, but at some point in my life (after I was born again) it occurred to me that the day the Lord told the Jews to keep holy was Saturday and not Sunday. As I thought about the fact that God does not make mistakes, I wondered why the Sabbath was changed to Sunday. In researching this, I found that Ignatius of Antioch approved non-observance of the Sabbath. More than likely, over time, as more and more gentiles came into the church, people simply did not feel the obligation to observe Jewish feast days or rituals.

Eventually, it became the custom of believers to assemble on the first day of the week – which is Sunday.

Then I reasoned, does it really matter? Saturday or Sunday? Mandatory or free will attendance? All I knew was that God loved me more than I could understand and I loved Him, so I wanted to spend time with His people, worshiping with them, hearing their testimonies, and learning more about God's Word and His will.

Resonating constantly was the fact that God loves me more than I can understand. He loves you and me just as much as He loves Abraham, Moses, or any of the other great heroes of the Bible, including the blessed Virgin Mary. He is the Creator of the entire universe with its billions of stars and galaxies, and He loves insignificant creatures like you and me. Amazing!

Missing Mass on any given Sunday will not cause you to lose your soul. God loves you far too much to judge you on such a small matter. He has a plan for all men and women to enter Heaven, and that includes you. Salvation does not come from following a bunch of rules that man thought to add to God's perfect plan. It's not Confession plus Mass and Communion plus not eating meat on Fridays plus doing good works plus tithing. It's not even following the Ten Commandments. It's very basic. In order to be saved, you just need Jesus. I know it may sound too easy, but that's exactly what God says. Remember: *"By grace you have been saved through faith, and this is not from yourselves, it is the gift from God."* (Ephesians 2:8 NIV) Getting to Heaven therefore is a gift. It comes from simply trusting what God says.

My favorite Bible verse (Proverbs 3:5) says, *"Trust in the Lord with all your heart and lean not on your own understanding; in all your ways acknowledge him and he will make your paths straight."* But man says, "That's too easy, I want to do something to help save my soul." Well, you don't have to trust what I say, but please trust the Bible.

Attached to the mandatory attendance at Mass is the issue of money! Whether it be in weekly tithes, purchasing of indulgences, or lighting candles, the Roman Catholic Church asks its members for a great deal of money each year. The church is worth a reported $30 billion, and yet there is a continuous call for more, more, more. For example, each year there is a call to donate to 'Peters Pence,' which has an annual goal of $55 million. Under church Law, and at the Pope's discretion, this money is available for the Pope's charitable donations. But guess what? According to the Wall Street Journal, only about 10 percent of that money makes it out the door.[10]

The Journal reported that the Vatican's deficit in 2018 doubled to more than $76 million, on a budget of approximately $333 million. A huge amount of that money went to pay off victims of clergy abuse, while another big chunk was lost to financial scandals. One recent scandal (in 2015) involved the Vatican's purchase of a bankrupt Italian hospital. Another scandal involved an investment of $100 million dollars, $60 million of that going to Rafael Mincionea, a long-time figure in Vatican finances. The latest scandal involved a global fund (Centurion) the Vatican used to invest millions of dollars into Hollywood films, energy projects, and European startups. All of these were bad investments that cost parishioners around the world dearly. The Vatican seems to have forgotten that the money it receives from church members must be considered a sacred trust. It should go to help the poor and needy in Jesus's name, and to share the good news of the gospel with those who have never heard it, not to make secular movies or fund private companies in Europe that have nothing to do with the gospel.

---

[10] The Wall Street Journal, December 11, 2019, "Vatican Uses Donations for the Poor to Plug Its Budget Deficit: Only 10% of donations to Peter's Pence collection go to charitable works," by Francis X. Rocca

The Church says that major investigations into these bad investments are underway, but past experience casts doubt on the belief that anything will ever come of them.

Indulgences

What are Indulgences? According to the Catholic Church, they bring about the remission of temporal punishment due to venial sins. In other words, you might think of them as being like the "Get out of Jail Free" card you get in the game of Monopoly. Only in the case of indulgences, they are not free. Far from it!

There are two different types of indulgences, Plenary (full remission), and Partial (remission for part of the punishment due for sin). In order to gain an indulgence, you must be in the state of grace. How does it work? Assume a loved one passed away and did not have any mortal sins charged against him. Remember, the Catholic Church teaches that there is no forgiveness for mortal sins. If you have committed any of these, you go straight to hell when you die, and stay there for all eternity. This is in contradiction to what Jesus Himself taught. He said that all sins can be forgiven except the blasphemy of the Holy Spirit—and He did not tell us exactly what he meant by this. (Matthew 12:31-32) So indulgences are considered to be only for those who have committed venial or minor sins, and who are suffering in Purgatory as a result.

This is wrong on many levels. First, as we've already seen, there is no Purgatory, no second chance. Your eternal state depends entirely upon whether you have surrendered your life to Jesus in this life and are thus clothed in His righteousness.

But Catholicism teaches that there is a Purgatory and that the Pope has personal control over what goes on there. He has granted to his priests the ability to use indulgences to shave time off the sentences of those who have been sent to Purgatory. These indulgences take advantage of merits earned through Christ's sufferings, Mary's good works, and all the good works accomplished by the saints.

The Church has the authority to release these merits and apply them to any person in Purgatory. I heard it explained that it is similar to early release from prison. Paroled early!

Where did this teaching about indulgences begin? In the Middle Ages, more than 1,000 years after the Resurrection of Jesus. In fact it was on November 27, 1095 that Pope Urban II called all Christians to go to war against Muslims in order to reclaim the Holy Land.

"Deus vult," he said. "God wills it."

The following year, the same Pope proclaimed that the Church now had control of the merit deposits that could bring about an early release from Purgatory. He went on to promise plenary indulgences to all who would participate in the Crusade to liberate the Holy Land from Muslim rule. It wasn't until nearly 250 years later that Pope Clement VI (1342-1352) proclaimed that the Pope himself had control of these deposits of merit. Soon thereafter the church began selling indulgences to people who wanted to spare their dead relatives from the pain of Purgatory. Millions of dollars came into the church coffers through this process, and beautiful, awe-inspiring cathedrals were built on the backs of the poor.

I can find nothing in the Bible to support the selling of indulgences. Nor do I find any teaching that anyone needs anything other than the blood of Jesus to be completely cleansed from his or her sins. As we discussed earlier, we are not saved by Jesus plus Mary plus the Saints. Christ alone saves us from our sins and protects us from the punishment we deserve. As Paul says in the third chapter of Romans:

> *"But now apart from the law the righteousness of God has been made known, to which the Law and the Prophets testify. **This righteousness is given through faith in Jesus Christ to all who believe.** (Emphasis mine) There is no difference between Jew and Gentile, for all have sinned and fall short of the glory of God, and all are justified freely by his grace through the redemption that came by Christ Jesus."* (Romans 3:21-24)

Paul also writes:

> *"Therefore, there is now no condemnation for those who are in Christ Jesus, because through Christ Jesus the law of the Spirit who gives life has set you free from the law of sin and death."* (Romans 8:1-2)

Where do indulgences fit in with what Paul says here? The answer is simple. They don't.

As Jesus said in John 5:24, *"Truly, Truly, he who hears My word, and believes Him who sent Me, has eternal life, and does not come into judgement, but has passed out of death into Life."*

Ritualism

Ritualism has long been at the core of Catholicism. Think of all the statues, candles, vestments, incense, and the dim lighting that is used to stir the senses of the parishioners. And there are so many breathtakingly beautiful cathedrals. To describe them as spectacular would be an understatement!

Consider the use of the crucifix. In the early church, Christians used a fish symbol to identify places of worship and Christian homes. Devotional art was also used, such as embroidered verses from the New Testament, crosses, and such.

If you read through the Law of Moses in the Old Testament, you will find that idolatry was forbidden. This was defined as the worship of images. The only exceptions to this can be found in Exodus 25:18-22, where God instructed Moses to carve Cherubim on the Ark of the Covenant, and in the following chapter (Exodus 26:3), where God said that figures of cherubim must be embroidered on the curtain that separates the Holy of Holies in the tabernacle tent.

Finally, Moses was commanded by God to build the Nehushtan, a bronze serpent that was lifted up on a pole. After Israelites were bitten by poisonous vipers in the desert, they were told that they would be healed if they looked upon the Nehushtan. (Numbers 21:4-9) According to most biblical scholars, the Nehushtan represented the cross and Christ being lifted up for our salvation. Thus, when the Israelites looked upon this pole, they were delivered from sin and death.

Although Exodus 20:4 forbids making idols, this serpent was not an idol. It was a symbol, sanctioned by God. Men, however, would idolize it until King Hezekiah broke it into pieces. It seems that many Israelites had burned incense to it. For some reason, people want to worship something they can see, but no image could come close to representing the majesty and glory of our God, who is beyond description.

The Scapular

Scapular means shoulders (from the Latin scapulae). It is a garment that is worn around the neck by a monk or a nun. One part rests on the wearer's back, and the front goes over the heart. The 'monastic scapular' initially appeared in the seventh century in the Order of St. Benedict. This was a large piece of cloth that went over the head and draped to the knees, similar to what present-day monks wear. The smaller 'devotional scapular' consists of two rectangular pieces of cloth. Special indulgences are available for those who wear this item. Over time, this garment became so important to the church that some members of religious orders were told to wear their scapulars at all times, even to bed at night. Some who failed to do this were excommunicated from the church.

The scapular is a pledge of motherly protection, not limited to this life but, supposedly, for the afterlife as well. According to Wikipedia, "The wearing of a devotional scapular has been viewed as a *constant meditation* by Bishop Leo De Goesbriand: "Wherever I am, whatever I am doing, Mary never sees me without seeing upon my body an evidence of my devotion to her."[11]

Wikipedia also says, "The fact that specific promises and indulgences were attached to the wearing of scapulars helped increase their following, as was seen with the early example of the Brown Scapular, habit of the Carmelites. This promise was based on the Carmelite tradition that the Blessed Virgin Mary appeared to St. Simon Stock at Cambridge, England in 1251 in answer to his appeal for help for his oppressed order and recommended the Brown Scapular of the Our Lady of Mount Carmel to him and promised salvation for the faithful who wore it piously."

And, "In the 1917 reported apparitions of Our Lady of Fátima the Virgin Mary is said to have appeared "with a Rosary in one hand and a scapular in the other". Sister Lúcia (one of the three Fátima children visionaries) stated that the Virgin Mary told her: "*The Rosary and the Scapular are inseparable.*"

Is the scapular approved by the Catholic Church? Absolutely, even though the Purple Scapular was introduced through a vision

---

[11] Pierre Chignon, "Meditations for the Use of the Secular Clergy," (Miami, FL; HardPress) 2017

to a stigmatist and mystic named Marie-Julie Jahenny. So what you have now in the church is a supernatural revelation given by an approved mystic.

Does it seem likely to you that Jesus Christ, who came to set people free—not only from sin and death, but from hundreds of religious rules set up by the Pharisees — would now bind His people with rules about what kind of clothes they should wear— even to bed at night? I believe such "holy" things detract the faithful from the true object of our worship, the Lamb who takes away the sins of the world.

I also believe this is one reason why many of the most holy religious relics have disappeared from public view. Where is the cross? God doesn't want us to know because He understands that we would turn it into an object of worship. And it is not the cross itself that should be venerated, but rather the One who shed his life's blood upon that cross. The same is true of the robe that Jesus wore. The cup He and His disciples used at the Last Supper. The sandals our Lord wore. Again, we are not to worship things, but God alone!

All of the things we've discussed in this chapter make up a small sampling of the ritualism that is incorporated into the modern catholic religion. Quite frankly, there is so much fantasy in what the church teaches that it can be difficult to separate fact from fiction.

In the book of Ephesians, Paul tells us how to quench the "fiery darts" of the wicked one. (Ephesians 6:16) He is making reference to ancient warfare, in which the enemy would launch dozens of 'fiery arrows' all at once. They seemed dangerous, and they sounded dangerous as they whistled through the sky — but they didn't cause a whole lot of damage. The soldiers on the receiving end of these attacks would simply hoist their shields above their heads and only a few would be injured.

This is basically what Satan does to us. He constantly hurls flaming lies at us. Some of his lies hit their mark. They take root and, over time, are accepted as fact. But their acceptance does not make them true. The solution to this predicament is to employ your shield of faith. If you are not walking out your faith by reading your Bible and praying every day, then you will become an easy mark for the adversary.

The answer to the question of how all this "stuff" found its way into the Catholic Church, is actually quite simple. Ecclesiastes 3:11 says of God, "He made everything beautiful in its time." We are also told that He put eternity into man's heart. This reference to eternity is basically God saying He built man with a button that says, "I am not supposed to die." Therefore, over the last two thousand years men have tried to keep their customs and beliefs alive by relaying them to their children. Thus, they passed along many of the "fiery darts" of Satan that had been accepted as fact. Thus, the demonic system has been carried down through the ages, and the festivals and ceremonies of pagan cultures have been incorporated into the church. In fact, much of what we see in the modern Catholic Church has come to us from ancient Babylonia. It is paganism and Christianity mixed together.

But as 2 Corinthians 6:14-15 says, *"For what partnership can righteousness have with wickedness? Or what fellowship does light have with darkness? What harmony is there between Christ and Belial? Or what does a believer have in common with an unbeliever? What agreement can exist between the temple of God and idols? For we are the temple of the living God."*

Chapter Five

What About the Rosary?

The Rosary is an item that takes people's eyes away from the finished work of Christ on the cross and places them squarely on his mother, Mary.

In case you are not familiar with the rosary, it is a series of beads, divided into five sections. Each of these sections contains one large bead followed by ten smaller beads. The large bead represents the "Our Father," or the Lord's Prayer. The remaining ten beads are connected to the "Hail Mary," which, of course, is found nowhere in the Bible. Thus, the rosary has ten times as many prayers to Mary as to our Heavenly Father. There is nothing here to remind the devout person of the death, burial and resurrection of Jesus Christ.

Again, it is basically a devotional to Mary. As a young man, I was completed caught up in devotion to the "mother of God," and repeated this prayer every night:

"O most beautiful flower of Mount Carmel, fruitful vine,

splendor of Heaven, blessed mother of the Son of God,

Immaculate virgin, assist me in my necessity. O star of the sea, help me herein and show me you are my mother. O holy Mary, mother of God, show me here you are my mother. O holy Mary, mother of God, queen of Heaven and earth, I humbly beseech you from the bottom of my heart to succor me in my request (this is where you insert your request.) There are none that can withstand thy power. O Mary, conceived without sin, pray for us who have recourse to thee (you say this three times). Holy Mary, I place this cause in your hands (again said three times)."

How does this prayer sync up to the Word of God?

First of all, the rosary represents a form of repetitive prayer that is condemned by Christ. In Matthew 6:7-8, He says:

"And when you pray, do not keep on babbling like pagans, for they think they will be heard because of their many words. Do not be like them, for your Father knows what you need before you ask him."

Most born-again believers use their own words when they pray, talking heart-to-heart with God as if He is their Father – which He is!

`Using beads of other tools to pray is reminiscent of what the Buddhists and Muslims used centuries before the rosary was invented. (Sati, the wife of Shiva, is described as being dressed in white and holding beads.) Notice I used the word, "invented," and I did it on purpose. The rosary was invented by a monk named Peter the Hermit in 1090 A.D. He was a Frenchman who preached during the Middle Ages. The rosary did not come into common use until over 100 years later, when it was reported that Mary appeared to St. Dominic in 1208 A.D., at the church of Prouille, and told him to pray the rosary and to teach others to do so.

After that, there have been many other reports of Mary's appearance. In all of these, Mary appeared as a ghost-like apparition – and her message was that God was calling His people to worship her. For example, Mary's message at Fatima in 1917 was "God wishes to establish in the world devotion to My immaculate heart. If this is done, then many souls will be saved and there will be peace!"

But Jesus said that there would be wars and rumors of wars until the day of His return. The Prophet Isaiah said that Jesus would be called, "The Prince of Peace." (Isaiah 9:6) And remember what Jesus said when He was told that His mother was waiting to talk to him: *"My mother and my brother are those who hear God's Word and put it into practice."* (Luke 8:21)

One final thought about the rosary and the glory it directs to Mary. Can you imagine God the Father saying to Jesus, "Son, you did a good job with mankind, but there are a few little details down there that I want your mother to go and deal with"? I can't. The Bible is clear that Jesus provided for our salvation when He went to the cross. He did not leave anything undone. This is why He cried out, "It is finished," just before He breathed His last. (John 19:30) The work of redemption was done. There was no need for a Co-Redemptress, as the Catholic Church calls her.

Yes, Mary is worthy of honor. She was chosen by God to carry and give birth to the Messiah. But Mary, like all of mankind, was a sinner. She learned more about her Holy Son and His mission as time went by. Unlike what you may have read from Catholic publications, she was not assumed to Heaven. Her life and public ministry were, by design, kept very quiet.

She never bragged or claimed sinlessness, nor did she make statements that she was the mother of God. More importantly, she never claimed to have any special power over God. She magnified the Lord and her spirit rejoiced in the Savior, Jesus Christ. As to how she really died, you will not find out until you get to Heaven yourself. Tradition has it that the apostle John was commissioned to take care of Christ's mother and that she eventually died at a ripe old age in the city of Ephesus. Now, you make your own mind up as to whether Mary made these after-death appearances on earth. Keep in mind that the devil's only interest is for you to take your eyes off Jesus and look at something else. Those who fix their eyes on these Marian apparitions are misguided and need to focus on Christ and what He accomplished.

`According to Catholic tradition there are 15 promises made regarding the rosary. For example, praying the rosary is supposed to give you special protection, cause virtue and good works to flourish in your life, and ensure that you will participate in the rewards of the saints in Heaven after you die. In fact, the Church says that those who pray the rosary will be delivered from Purgatory and receive a high degree of glory in heaven.

Many of the 15 rosary promises are restatements of promises that Jesus made to all who follow Him. As we've said several times before, faith in Jesus is all sufficient. Nothing else is needed for reconciliation with God or for eternal life.

For example, Jesus promises that those who believe in Him will never die. But now, it seems the church is teaching that those who believe in Jesus and pray the rosary will never die.

The Bible says that anyone who believes in Jesus has already passed from death to life and will live forever in Heaven. John 3:16 tells us, *"For God so loved the world that he gave his one and only Son, that whoever believes in him shall not perish but have eternal life."* But now, apparently, we are told that we need the rosary <u>plus</u> Jesus to "participate in the rewards of the saints in Heaven."

The church says that if you pray the rosary, whatever you ask God for will be given to you, but Jesus already told us, *"You may ask for anything in my name and I will do it."* (John 14:14)

Jesus is sufficient. He is all we need. Nothing else is required. As the book of Galatians says, *"Evidently some people are throwing you into confusion and are trying to pervert the gospel of Christ. But even if we or an angel from Heaven should preach a gospel other than the one we preached to you, let them be under God's curse! As we have already said, so now I say again: If anybody is preaching to you a gospel other than what you accepted, let them be under God's curse!"* (Galatians 1:7-9)

CHAPTER SIX

WILL I GO TO PURGATORY?

According to the teachingS of the Roman Catholic Church, Purgatory is a holding place for imperfect Christians who are not ready for Heaven when they die, but not quite sinful enough to be cast into hell. The souls who are assigned to Purgatory have committed venial sins, of course. No one who has committed a mortal sin is allowed to enter. The former are to suffer in Purgatory until all sin has been purged away. As a matter of fact, according to the teachings of the Roman Catholic Church, very few people go straight to Heaven when they die, even if they have surrendered their lives to Christ and accepted His sacrifice on the cross for the forgiveness for their sins.

When I was a boy, I was told that God forgives sin, but that His justice requires full punishment before anyone is allowed into Heaven. I felt that people I knew who had passed away were now in agony in the flames of Purgatory. I prayed for them constantly, but that did little to relieve the sorrow I felt, knowing they were suffering in this way.

The church also taught that, in addition to praying for your loved ones in Purgatory, you could help them by buying indulgences, which supposedly brought relief from pain. The selling of indulgences was one of the reasons why Martin Luther rebelled against the teachings of the Roman Catholic Church. Luther said that the selling of indulgences drew believers away from the one true source of salvation, which was faith in Christ. When Luther insisted that God alone had the power to forgive sins, the pontifical council ordered him to retract his claims immediately, but he refused.

Back in that time, the church used high-pressure tactics to sell indulgences, such as asking parishioners to put their hands near a flame so they would have a clearer understand of the pain their loved ones were enduring. Many poor families were pushed deeper into poverty through buying indulgences to alleviate their loved ones' suffering.

Think about this. A Christian dies and Christ comes to usher him into Heaven. Now, a Roman Catholic dies, and he or she is met by who knows who or what, to be ushered into Purgatory.

There is no comfort for the family members left behind because they know that mom, or dad, or their beloved aunt or uncle, is now in a place of torment. It may not be hell – because it won't last for all eternity – but otherwise the two places are interchangeable. But the good news is that Purgatory does not really exist.

The Bible teaches that those who belong to Christ will pass immediately into Paradise when they die. Those who do not belong to Christ will be sent immediately to hell.

The Bible also says that Jesus was crucified between two thieves, one on each side of him. One of thieves joined in with those who were mocking Jesus and sarcastically urging Him to come down from the cross and save Himself. The other knew the Lord was an innocent, godly man and asked, "Jesus, remember me when you come into your kingdom." Jesus replied, "Truly I tell you, today you will be with me in Paradise." (Luke 23:42-43)

This man was most likely a common criminal who had lived all his life in sin. He even admitted that he and the other thief deserved the . But in an instant, Jesus forgave Him and promised him that he would soon be in Paradise. If Jesus showed such kindness and love to a man who had spent his life as a criminal, then surely He will do the same for you – and me.

You may also remember Jesus's parable of the rich man and Lazarus. The rich man was apparently a cold-hearted fellow who enjoyed the best of everything while a beggar named Lazarus suffered just outside the walls of his estate. Jesus said:

"The time came when the beggar died and the angels car-
ried him to Abraham's side. The rich man also died and was
buried. In Hades, where he was in torment, he looked up
and saw Abraham far away, with Lazarus by his side. So
he called to him, 'Father Abraham, have pity on me and
send Lazarus to dip the tip of his finger in water and cool
my tongue, because I am in agony in this fire.'

"But Abraham replied, 'Son, remember that in your lifetime you received your good things, while Lazarus received bad things, but now he is comforted here and you are in agony. And besides all this, between us and you a great chasm has been set in place, so that those who want to go from here to you cannot, nor can anyone cross over from there to us.'" *(Luke 16:22-26)*

Abraham did not try to comfort the rich man by telling him, "You won't have to suffer very long. Once your sins have been dealt with you'll come up here to be with us." He wasn't in a holding station, but in hell itself.

The Roman Catholic Church teaches that the sufferings in purgatory vary but, according to Bellarmine, a Catholic theologian, the pain of hell is felt in Purgatory. And, according to St. Thomas Aquinas, "The least pain in purgatory, surpasses the greatest suffering in this life." In essence, this doctrine enhances the "Fear Factor" inherent in Catholicism.

But again, remember that Purgatory does not really exist. As Jesus said, *"Very truly I tell you, whoever hears my word and believes him who sent me has eternal life and will not be judged but has crossed over from death to life."* (John 5:24)

You may be wondering, since Purgatory does not exist, where does this notion come from? The Greek philosopher Plato who, of course, lived several hundred years before Christ, was a Proponent of this idea.

So was Alexander the Great, who spread the idea of a place of temporary punishment after death throughout the Greek empire, where it eventually reached the Jews. The Rabbis then began teaching children that their offerings would alleviate their parents' suffering. The Rabbis also introduced a theory which divided the underworld into two realms. These were Paradise, a place of happiness, and Gehenna, a place of torment.

The apostle Peter wrote, *"For Christ also suffered once for sins, the righteous for the unrighteous, to bring you to God. He was put to death in the body but made alive in the Spirit."* (1 Peter 3:18)

In other words, Christ is bringing us to God. This means that we cannot be made to suffer for sin a second time. So, the bottom line is Purgatory is a man-made Hoax!

Praise God, we don't have to suffer to be cleansed from sin. Christ took our sins upon Himself and suffered in our behalf. The Bible teaches that being right before a holy God is not a process. It comes by faith, and faith alone!

CHAPTER SEVEN

IS THERE ANYTHING HOLY ABOUT THAT WATER?

Y ou don't have to be a Roman Catholic to know about holy water. If you're a fan of old horror movies, you know how effective holy water can be when it comes to battling vampires. Sprinkle some holy water on those fanged creatures of the night, and it burns through them like acid. Just watch as they disintegrate into nothingness.

Come to think of it, though, water was also what Dorothy used to kill the Wicked Witch in *The Wizard of Oz*. And in M Night Shyamalan's movie *Signs*, it was water that killed the evil aliens. (Since water was deadly to them, those aliens had to be more than a little stupid to come to a planet where two-thirds of the surface is covered by water.) And that was just regular water. Nothing holy about it at all, except that God created it, just as He created everything in the universe.

Now, just in case someone misunderstands me, I want to make it clear that I don't really believe in horror stories or fairy tales. I am not carrying around a canteen of holy water in cases I run into a vampire, a wicked witch or a bunch of space aliens.

But the truth is that the concept of holy water can be traced back to ancient times, where the priest would wash his hands in preparation for worship. In some traditions, the mixture of water and salt symbolized the brine of the sea. In the Wicca religion, this was representative of the womb of the goddess, which was considered to be the source of all life on earth. This water-salt mixture was consecrated and used in many religious ceremonies and magical rituals.

The use of holy water in Christianity dates back to the time of the apostles, where it was used for purification purposes. In the Middle Ages, holy water was considered sacred, so much so that churches had to keep their fountains locked up to keep people from stealing the water.

Many religions use sacred water. For example:

- In Hinduism, water represents God in a spiritual sense, and bathing in the Ganges River is considered to be sacred.
- Buddhists use water in many of their religious ceremonies.
- Muslims drink blessed water for healing purposes.
- As I've already mentioned Wiccans use salt and water combinations for religious ceremonies and magic rituals.

Without water there is no life. Water then is a symbol of life. So the question must be asked: Is believing in Holy Water good or bad?

Since the Bible is the only place for truthfulness let's review what it tells us. In point of fact, holy water is mentioned directly in the book of Numbers 5:17 "...and the priest shall take 'Holy Water' in an earthenware vessel; and he shall take some of the dust that is on the floor of the tabernacle and put it into water." (Numbers 5:17) In this instance, the water was used in a ritual to determine whether a woman was guilty of committing adultery. If the woman was innocent, she would experience no ill effects from drinking this bitter water. If she was guilty, the water would cause her to be cursed.

In Exodus, the Lord tells Moses to make a bronze basin, place it between the tent of meeting and the altar, and put water in it. Aaron and his sons were then to wash their hands and feet with water from it before they entered the tabernacle. If they failed to do this, they would die. This was to be an everlasting ordinance. (Exodus 40:30-32)

The truth is that there is holiness in water only if and because God places it there. Water has no power of its own. Even when we are baptized, it is not the power of the water that cleanses us, but rather the fact that baptism itself is a symbol of the death, burial and resurrection of Jesus Christ. Again, our faith cannot be in "holy water," but in the saving power of our Lord.

Chapter Eight

Pope Francis on Same Sex Relationships

A s we have seen, one of the major differences between the Roman Catholic and Protestant churches is that the former teaches that church traditions are on the same level with the teachings that are contained in the Bible. Catholics also consider the Pope to be the leader of the worldwide church, and thus, God's spokesman on earth. Although he is only considered to be infallible when he is speaking "ex cathedra," anything he says at any time is accepted as authoritative by most Catholic believers.

And that's a problem when His words contradict what the Bible teaches. This was the case in October of 2020 when Pope Francis spoke out on same-sex relationships. On October 21, CNN reported, "Pope endorses civil union laws for same-sex couples."

According to the Catholic News Agency, the Pope said, "Homosexuals are children of God and have a right to a family." He went on to say, "Nobody should be thrown out, or be made miserable because of it. What we have to create is a civil union law. That way they are legally covered."

What does the Bible say about this controversial subject?

In the book of Romans, Paul writes, that because people had turned against God, "God gave them over to shameful lusts. Even their women exchanged natural sexual relations for unnatural ones. In the same way the men also abandoned natural relations with women and were inflamed with lust for one another. Men committed shameful acts with other men and received in themselves the due penalty for their error. Furthermore, just as they did not think it worthwhile to retain the knowledge of God, so God gave them over to a depraved mind, so that they do what ought not to be done." (Romans 1:26-28)

In the Old Testament, Leviticus 13:20 says, *"If a man has sexual relations with a man as one does with a woman, both of them have done what is detestable. They are to be put to death; their blood will be on their own heads."*

It seems clear to me from these passages that God abhors homosexual behavior. I may not like what the Bible says about it. Even those who find homosexual practices abhorrent may feel compassion toward those who are caught up in the homosexual lifestyle. But how we feel and what we think doesn't matter. We can't say that same-sex unions are okay with God because they're clearly not.

When God speaks, His church must obey.

We also know that God does not change His mind. He doesn't pronounce that something is wrong and then decide that it's really okay—as the Roman Catholic Church did about eating meat on Friday.

So why did the Pope feel compelled to say what he did about same-sex marriages? Even though I believe that what he said was wrong, I hope it was because he has a compassionate heart. But I must admit that I've wondered if it had anything at all to do with money. After all, the COVID-19 pandemic has brought about a huge drop in revenue. Having Sunday mass on Zoom cannot possibly be as lucrative as having it in a church filled with believers. Inviting gay couples into the church—telling them that they can be members in good-standing without changing their lifestyle— would certainly increase the number of Catholics around the world (and thus bring in more money every Sunday).

The Bible tells us that when God created the first human beings, He made them male and female. Sex is His invention. He planned for marriage to be between one man and one woman who come together as one flesh. There are no other options. I have heard it said that God created Adam and Eve, not Adam and Steve, and that is absolutely true.

Bear in mind that there is nothing new about homosexuality. Apparently, it was practiced among the ancient Hebrews. If not, why would God prohibit it in the Law of Moses? Actually, same sex unions were known in many parts of the ancient world.

In fact, thirteen of the first fourteen emperors in Rome were bi-sexual or homosexual. Nero, for example, married two men. In his first marriage, to Pythagoras, he was the bride. In his second, to Sporus, he was the groom. Many examples of same-sex unions are also found in Ancient Greece. One notable union was between Alexander and Hephaestion. Sexual perversion is nothing new.

Now, I want you to know that being attracted to a member of your own sex is not a sin. It is acting on the temptation that is the problem. This is a sin that God refers to as an abomination. Even so, God loves all sinners. His grace is open to gay and straight people alike. His forgiveness is readily available to those who repent and turn from their sins.

I know I have deviated from the topic at hand here, which is that we must be obedient to the laws of God rather than the traditions of men. But the discussion of same-sex relationships is important, and I think that Pope Francis may have caused serious harm when he talked about same-sex couples being part of God's family. It frightens me to think that some who are caught up in this would think that the Pope has given them God's blessing and license to continue in their sins. How terrible to think that any should be lost because of this.

Jesus actually spoke out against the traditions of men on several occasions. For example, He did this when He did not wash His hands according to the 'traditions' of the second temple period. (Matthew 15:1-9) And when he healed a crippled man on the Sabbath. (Matthew 12:9-13) Also, when he and his disciples plucked corn to eat as they walked through the fields on the Sabbath Day. (Matthew 12:1-8) And then, in the seventh chapter of Mark, He really let us know how he feels about man-made traditions being disguised as God's laws:

He replied, "Isaiah was right when he prophesied about you
hypocrites; as it is written:
"'These people honor me with their lips,
but their hearts are far from me.
They worship me in vain;
their teachings are merely human rules.'
You have let go of the commands of God and are holding on
to human traditions."

And he continued, "You have a fine way of setting aside
the commands of God in order to observe your own tradi-
tions! For Moses said, 'Honor your father and mother,' and,
'Anyone who curses their father or mother is to be put to
death.' But you say that if anyone declares that what might
have been used to help their father or mother is Corban (that
is, devoted to God)—then you no longer let them do any-
thing for their father or mother. Thus you nullify the word
of God by your tradition that you have handed down. And
you do many things like that." (Mark 7:6-13)

As I'm sure you know, Joshua was a great leader of Israel, the suc-
cessor of Moses. In the 24th chapter of the book that bears his name,

he speaks to the children of Israel as they are about to begin their new life in the Promised Land:

> *"Now fear the LORD and serve him with all faithfulness. Throw away the gods your ancestors worshiped beyond the Euphrates River and in Egypt, and serve the LORD. But if serving the LORD seems undesirable to you, then choose for yourselves this day whom you will serve, whether the gods your ancestors served beyond the Euphrates, or the gods of the Amorites, in whose land you are living. But as for me and my household, we will serve the Lord." (Joshua 24:14-15)*

We must choose to serve the Lord. We cannot go chasing after ancient gods, which seems to me to be what the leadership of the Roman Catholic Church has done. My studies have led me to see how many of the rituals and ceremonies of Catholicism are derived from pagan practices that originated in ancient Babylon, as well as other countries that faded into "the dustbin of history" many centuries ago.

Am I saying that all Catholics are lost? Not at all. I know many fine Catholics who have surrendered their lives to Jesus and will be spending eternity in Heaven with Him – beyond any doubt. But I also know some who have never given a thought to their relationship with Christ. They seem to think, "I'm okay, spiritually. The church is taking care of that." But the church can't do that for you. Your salvation is based on a personal relationship with Jesus, and if you don't have that, you don't have anything!

As I said, there will be many Catholics in Heaven, but they will get there the same way everyone else does – by trusting in God and the provision He has made.

You can't get to Heaven by following man-made rules, but simply understanding that there is no entrance but through Christ. I realize that I may be repeating myself here. But that's because this is so important, and I want to make sure it is understood completely. No one gets to Heaven by "doing," but by "trusting." James 2:19 says, "You believe there is one God. Good! Even demons believe that; and shudder." Faith is more than just believing God exists. It is having a close relationship with Him.

Thinking back on my life, I remember many relatives who seldom or never read their Bibles. Many have passed on, and it makes me sad to think that I may never see them ever again. But then I read, *"Yet to all who did receive him, to those who believed in his name, he gave the right to become children of God—children born not of natural descent, nor of human decision or a husband's will, but born of God."*

This is great news for all the Catholic brethren who do not adhere to all the rituals and laws mandated by the church. Always remember:

"Trust in what God said, not what man says!"

Most of us ask at one time or another, "What is God's will for me?" The answer is that God's Word is His will. Therefore, read your Bible. If you are living in obedience to the precepts found in the Bible, whatever you ask for in prayer will be granted. If you are uncertain what His Word says on any subject, then your ability to withstand the spiritual warfare that awaits mankind will cripple you. The Apostle Paul warns us:

> *"For our struggle is not against flesh and blood, but against the rulers and authorities of the unseen world, against mighty powers in this dark world and against the spiritual forces of evil in the Heavenly realms." (Ephesians 6:12)*

Most of us are aware that Cain and Abel were the first two children born into this world after the creation of humankind. We know, too, that Cain was the world's first murderer, killing his brother in a jealous rage. But let's look a little bit deeper.

Cain was a farmer, who worked hard to raise an abundant crop of grains and vegetables.

Abel, on the other hand, was a shepherd, who watched over healthy flocks of sheep.

After a year of success, both brothers naturally wanted to thank the Lord for how He had blessed them. The Bible says:

> *"In the course of time Cain brought some of the fruits of the soil as an offering to the LORD. And Abel also brought an*

offering—fat portions from some of the firstborn of his flock. The LORD looked with favor on Abel and his offering, but on Cain and his offering he did not look with favor. So Cain was very angry, and his face was downcast.

"Then the LORD said to Cain, 'Why are you angry? Why is your face downcast? If you do what is right, will you not be accepted? But if you do not do what is right, sin is crouching at your door; it desires to have you, but you must rule over it.'

"Now Cain said to his brother Abel, 'Let's go out to the field.' While they were in the field, Cain attacked his brother Abel and killed him." (Genesis 4:3-8)

Bible scholars give a number of possible reasons why Cain's sacrifice was not pleasing to God.

I believe the most likely reason was that Cain presented the wrong type of sacrifice. In looking ahead to Jesus's sacrifice on the cross of Calvary, God had already let it be known that there is no forgiveness without the shedding of blood. (Hebrews 9:22) God required a blood sacrifice, and Cain had not met this requirement.

Another possible reason for God's acceptance of Abel's sacrifice and rejection of Cain's may have been that Abel gave the first-fruits of His flock, whereas Cain brought in the leftover produce that didn't quite make the grade. I admit, there is no evidence that this was the case, but it is plausible. And isn't it interesting how often God stood up for the disregarded little brother? Abel over Cain, Jacob over Esau, David over his bigger, stronger brothers. Don't get me wrong. I know that God loves brothers (and sisters) equally, no matter where they were born into their families. But in a society that valued first-born children above all others, God showed from the very beginning that he was not concerned about such traditions and rituals. He looked at a person's character rather than his rank in the family.

Whatever the specific cause of God's rejection may have been, it seems clear that Abel understood what God wanted, and gave Him what He had asked for, whereas Cain figured He could do whatever He wanted, and that would be fine with God.

Not so! God must be obeyed.

More than likely, both brothers brought their offerings to the tree of life, but were thwarted by the cherubim who guarded the tree. (Cherubim are always associated with God. See Exodus 25:10-22.)

Apparently, Cain was making an offering because He knew it was expected and He wanted to be in favor with God. Able offered up his offering because He had a thankful heart. The older brother was trusting in "works" to save Him, whereas Abel was acting in faith. Hebrews 11:4 tells us "By faith Abel offered up a more excellent sacrifice than Cain."

I have an important question. How did Abel get to Heaven? How about Cain? The answer is that they both got there – assuming Cain was saved – the same way everyone else has since the first day of Creation: By faith! After all, there was no mass for them to attend. No priest to confess to. There was no sacrament called "communion" and the cross hadn't even happened yet. They got to Heaven by faith. By simply trusting in God.

Proverbs 3:5 tells us to *"Trust in the Lord with all your heart, and do not lean on your own understanding."*

This is exactly what God expects us to do!

Most Catholics think that following the rules will get them into Heaven. That's what I thought when I was a Catholic, and it's what Cain thought when he was one of the first few people on earth: "I worked very hard to produce this crop. I followed all the protocols. I spent many hours watching and watering. I harvested, I transported, and eventually I delivered it to my God. But He rejected it for a bloody calf my brother brought. Notice all the "I's."

Cain misunderstood. We are required only to have faith, trust in God and do what He says.

As we have already seen, there are many Catholic traditions that conflict with the biblical truth that we are saved by faith and faith alone. We do not have to pray the rosary, demonstrate our devotion to the saints, wear the scapular, believe in the assumption of Mary, etc.

I've had devoted Catholics tell me that all these traditions can be traced back to the teachings of Jesus, but this is not true. Can you imagine Christ teaching His followers to pray the rosary, especially since He taught His disciples to pray the "Our Father?"

Each of the practices mentioned above can be traced to a specific time when it became part of Roman Catholic theology. For example, in

1546 the Council of Trent declared that the Word of God is contained both in Scripture and Tradition — that the two are equal in authority, and that every Catholic is required to give equal veneration to both! Really? Try all you will to research all these so-called traditions and you will not find any scriptural basis. What you will find is silence. A great example of this is the papacy itself. The Bible has nothing to say about the Pope and his leadership role in the Church. But it has much to say regarding how much God hates it when statues are used in worship!

One of the things that happened at the Council of Trent was that the second of the Ten Commandments was dropped from the list, and the original ninth commandment was split, thereby keeping the number of commandments at ten.

Why was the second commandment dropped? Because by this time, the Catholic Church was deeply committed to its use of statues and images. The bishops knew that the church's practices did not match up with what the Bible taught. But rather than change what the church was doing, they decided to change the Bible instead! But there are many other scriptures that show God's opposition to idols.

> **Leviticus 26:1:** *"You shall not make idols for yourselves or erect an image or pillar, and you shall not set up a figured stone in your land to bow down to it, for I am the Lord your God."*

Deuteronomy 27:15: *"Cursed is the man who makes an idol or a molten image, an abomination to the Lord, the work of the hands of the craftsman, and sets it up in secret."*

1 John 5:21: *"Little children guard yourselves from idols."*

Why does God feel so strongly about statues? Because He knows that whenever a statue is used to represent a religious figure, it is not long until people are worshiping the statue as if it were the person or object it represents. This seems to be human nature. We need something to look at, but no image could ever begin to represent the majesty of our invisible God.

When Moses went up on the mountain to get the Ten Commandments, he was gone so long that the Israelites began to worry that something had happened to him and that he wasn't coming back. Even though they knew that God had led them out of Egypt, that wasn't enough for them. They had seen the fire by night and the pillar of smoke during the day, leading them ever onward toward the Promised Land, but that wasn't enough either. They wanted to worship a God they could see.

When Moses finally came down from the mountain, he found the Israelites worshiping a calf made of gold, fashioned by his brother Aaron out of the people's melted-down jewelry. Ironically, the second of the Ten Commandments was, "You shall not make for yourself an image in the form of anything in Heaven above or on the earth beneath or in the waters below. You shall not bow down to them or worship them..."

The people were severely punished for their transgression, and thousands died.

And yet, as the philosopher George Santayana said, "Those who cannot remember the past are condemned to repeat it."

Sure enough, the "golden calf episode" was repeated about 150 years later, after a man named Gideon had led the Israelites in a war against the occupying Midianites. After the battle had been won, the people wanted to make Gideon ruler over their newly liberated nation. Gideon refused this honor, but he did accept a gift from each of the families – one golden earring that had been plundered from their enemies. The Bible says:

> *"So they spread out a garment, and each of them threw a ring from his plunder onto it. The weight of the gold rings he asked for came to seventeen hundred shekels, not counting the ornaments, the pendants and the purple garments worn by the kings of Midian or the chains that were on their camels' necks. Gideon made the gold into an ephod, which he placed in Ophrah, his town. All Israel prostituted themselves by worshiping it there, and it became a snare to Gideon and his family.* (Judges 8:24-27)

You may think that looking at an image, such as Christ on a crucifix, helps you focus your prayers and remember Who you are praying to. But it is easy to cross over the line and began worshiping the statue, even though you may not realize that this is what you are doing.

When I was a kid, we sometimes played a game we called "Whisper." You probably played it too. Here's how it worked: A group of kids would get in a line. The boy or girl at the front of the line would whisper something to the next person in line. He or she would whisper it to the next child in line, and so on, until the message reached the end of the line. At that point, the last child to hear the message would say it out loud to the entire group. Then, the one who gave the original message would share what he had actually said.

Usually, by the time the whispered message had made its way through six or seven kids, it was completely unrecognizable. The laughs came because the final message almost always had nothing in common with how it had started out. In fact, I can't remember a single time where the original message didn't change drastically.

This small "house game" is a good example of how things get twisted in the telling. Imagine how oral traditions have changed as they have been handed down over centuries. Something is always lost in translation, and it's almost always something important.

This is just one more reason why the Bible – the written Word of God — is the arbiter in matters of faith and morals.

Earlier in this book, we talked about author David B. Currie and his conversion to Catholicism. To defend his belief that oral traditions are equal in importance to Scripture, He cites 2 Thessalonians 2:15, "*So then, brothers, stand firm and hold to the teachings we passed on to you, whether by word of mouth or by letter.*" He also mentions Paul's instruction to Timothy, *"And the things you have heard me say in the presence of many witnesses entrust to reliable people who will also be qualified to teach others."* (2 Timothy 2:2)

Where I believe Mr. Currie goes astray is in his understanding of Paul's view of tradition. In these passages, he is referring to the essential truths of the gospel. These are the basics: That Christ shed His blood on the cross to pay the penalty for the sins of all mankind, that he was buried, came back to life on the third day, and ascended into Heaven where He reigns forever at the right-hand of God. These truths were delivered by Christ Himself to the apostles, delivered by the apostles to the church, and by the church to the rest of the world. The Apostles also delivered the ordinances of the gospels, such as baptism and the Lord's Supper. There were no hidden rituals or ceremonies that only the faithful would know. God wants everyone to understand the gospel message in all its simplicity, yet glory and power.

At the Last Supper with His apostles, before He was betrayed and arrested, Jesus told them:

"As the Father has loved me, so have I loved you. Now remain in my love. If you keep my commands, you will remain in my love, just as I have kept my Father's commands and remain in his love. I have told you this so that my joy may be in you and that your joy may be complete. My command is this: Love each other as I have loved you. Greater love has no one than this: to lay down one's life for one's friends."

Jesus said His command is that we love each other as He has loved us. He did not add, "And pray the rosary...worship my mother, Mary... pray to all the saints...wear the scapula...and on and on. His yoke is easy and His burden is light!

Over fifty years ago the Beatles had a big hit song that said, "All you need is love." They had it wrong. All you need is Jesus.

CHAPTER NINE

WHY DOES ALL THIS MATTER, ANYWAY?

G enesis, the first book of the Bible, tells us that God formed man from the dust from the ground, and placed him in the Garden of Eden. God also commanded Adam not to eat the fruit of the majestic tree that stood in the center of the garden—the tree of the knowledge of good and evil. When God said that it was not good for Adam to be alone—despite the fact that he had plenty of animal companion-ship—God created another human being. The first woman, Eve, was presented to Adam as his companion and helper.

The first humans were having a wonderful time in the Garden of Eden. They were completely contented and had everything they needed to be satisfied and happy, including enough work to give them a sense of purpose. God had told them to take care of all the trees and other plants in the garden, and that was a pretty nice job, considering that there were no weeds, thistles, or plant diseases of any kind. Neither were there fleas, ticks or any other irritating insects or bacteria to bother the animals.

But then Satan came along in the form of a serpent.

He pointed out to the woman that there were some big, juicy, delicious-looking fruit hanging on the tree of the knowledge of good and evil. Eve stared at that luscious-looking fruit and her mouth began to water.

The serpent asked her, "Has God told you not to eat the fruit from this tree?"

She admitted this was true. God said that she and her partner could eat from any other tree in the garden, but not this one. They weren't even supposed to touch it. In fact, God had said that if she and Adam ate the fruit from this tree, they would "surely die."

No one had ever died before this, so I'm not even sure that Eve knew what it meant. But from the way God said it, she knew it was something terrible.

Satan pooh-poohed this. He told her that God was being jealous. "He just said that because He knows that if you eat from the tree you'll be just like Him. Your eyes will be opened and you'll know the difference between good and evil." He kept on like this until Eve was convinced.

She took a few big bites of the fruit, and it *was* delicious, just like the snake said. "Adam," she said, "you just have to try some of this."

He did, and as the serpent had said would happen, their eyes were opened and they knew the difference between good and evil. But at the same time, sin and death entered the world, along with weeds, viruses, thistles, pain, sorrow, sickness, and all sorts of trouble.

But from the very beginning, God had a plan to restore His relationship with humankind. That plan involved sending His only Son to give Himself as the perfect sacrifice for our sins.

He told the serpent, *"I will put enmity between you and the woman and between your offspring and hers; he will crush your head, and you will strike his heel."* (Genesis 3:15) This is a prophecy that Christ will overcome Satan through His death, burial and resurrection.

There is another parallel here as well. Before Adam and Eve ate the forbidden fruit, they had no sense of shame. They were naked as they worked together in the garden, and never gave it a second thought. The weather was just right, so they never needed clothing to shelter them from the cold. There were no stickers to step on, or sharp rocks to cut their feet, so they didn't need shoes.

But after they ate the fruit, they suddenly realized that they were naked, so they hid. They were also ashamed that they had disobeyed, and this was another reason they didn't want God to see them. The Bible says, "The Lord made garments of skin for Adam and his wife and clothed them." Of course, this meant that two animals had to die in order to cover up Adam and Eve's shame.

Once again, this event looks forward to Jesus's death, burial and resurrection. Only those who are clothed in His righteousness are able to enter into Heaven and live forever with God. As he said, *"I am the way, the truth and the life. No one comes to the Father except through me."* (John 14:6)

In the 22nd chapter of Matthew, Jesus told a parable about a king who prepared a wedding banquet for his son. When the day of the wedding came, all the people he had invited essentially thumbed their noses at him. For some reason, they all felt that they had better things to do. The king responded by sending his servants out into all the nearby towns and villages and inviting everyone to come, and they filled the banquet hall. (Can there be any doubt that Jesus was talking about the Jewish people's refusal to accept Him as the Messiah, and God's mercy being extended to the gentiles – people like you and me – as a result.

But that's not the end of the story, On the day of the wedding, the king noticed that one of the new invitees had come to the banquet without wearing the proper clothes. The Bible says:

"But when the king came in to see the guests, he noticed a man there who was not wearing wedding clothes. He asked, 'How did you get in here without wedding clothes, friend?' The man was speechless.

"Then the king told the attendants, 'Tie him hand and foot, and throw him outside, into the darkness, where there will be weeping and gnashing of teeth.'

"For many are invited, but few are chosen."

You see, we are all invited to the banquet, but we had better show up wearing the righteousness that comes only through faith in Christ! If not, we too will be cast into outer darkness.

Unfortunately, after sin came into the world, human beings were increasingly drawn to it. Over several hundred years, it reached the point where "every inclination of the thoughts of the human heart was only evil all the time." (Genesis 6:5)

In His wisdom, God decided to start over again, using a great flood to destroy everyone on earth, except for a righteous man named Noah, his wife, and their three sons and daughters-in-law.

There were many people on earth prior to the flood. William Whiston estimates that the our planet had a population of around 500 million people.[12] One writer has estimated Adam could have seen over a million of his own descendants, based on the fact that he lived to be 930 years old. But God destroyed them all, except for the eight members of Noah's family.

Why did God choose Noah and his family to survive the flood and repopulate the earth? Noah was chosen because he was obedient to God. When he sinned, as we all do, he confessed his sin to the Lord, and was forgiven. As John 1:9 tells us, *"If we confess our sins, he is faithful and just and will forgive us our sins and purify us from all unrighteousness."*

---

[12] Whiston was a mathematician and Anglican priest whose book, "A New Theory of the Earth," was published in 1696.

After the flood, God instructed Noah and the other members of his family to "be fruitful and multiply," and they did exactly as He said. Soon there were a number of different people groups living in different parts of the world.

One of the important leaders during this time was a man named Nimrod. Nimrod was mighty on this earth. It is believed that he ruled over Babel, which was the first organized rebellion by the human race against God. (See Genesis 11:1-9). The name Nimrod literally means "Let us rebel." Why am I telling you all of this? Simply to give you a picture of life, and especially the religious life of this time. Even though the flood had destroyed a wicked and disobedient race of people, things were not a whole lot better on the new earth. Nimrod represented the self-centered, bullying type who cared only about himself and I'm afraid that he was the norm. The Bible says that during these early days of the reborn world, "every man did what was right in his own eyes." (Judges 21:25)

In other words, men and women created their own beliefs, and went their own way. So how did man get to Heaven during this very self-centered period? The answer is, the same way that you and I will. It's a timeless principle. *"The righteous shall live by faith."* (Habakkuk 2:4) They got to Heaven the same way the thief on the cross did, the same way Abraham did, the same way everyone who will ever go to Heaven will – by trusting in God and His Holy Word. An important part of faith is knowing that God's Word is all you need. You can't depend on religious ceremonies, or a list of do's and don'ts. Heaven is not something to be earned or worked for. It is a gift, and all we have to do is receive it. I realize that I have said this same thing many times in the course of this book. But that's only because it is so important! It is imperative that you accept the gift of eternal life Jesus offers.

To my Catholic brothers and sisters I say, *"Be alert and of sober mind. Your enemy the devil prowls around like a roaring lion looking for someone to devour."* – 1 Peter 5:8

Please don't let your life get bogged down with "man-made" rules. Jesus wants us to rest in what He did on the cross. The great evangelist Billy Graham was once asked what the biggest surprise of his life had been. He replied, "The brevity of it." Life is short, so make sure you use it wisely.

God is not interested in our pleasures. He knows that the devil uses the things of this world, especially sex, to get us to stop thinking about the Lord. Your daily walk must never exclude the Holy Spirit. Consider all the ways people give in to the temptations the devil throws at them. Some choose money over God. Others grab for the pleasures of sin or chase after power and fame. But all of these ultimately disappoint and leave those who seek them feeling abandoned and alone. You see, without God, we have nothing of value. Please stay on guard. Remember that we all begin eternity the moment we are born. We must choose our paths carefully.

CHAPTER TEN

AVOIDING THE TRICKS OF THE DEVIL

I n the last chapter, we talked about the fact that ever since the first humans were created, the righteous have always lived by faith.

Conversely, since his first encounter with the human race, the devil has used specific techniques to try to seduce us away from our faith relationship with God.

The Apostle John puts it this way:

"For all that is in the world, the lust of the flesh, and the lust of the eyes, and the boastful pride of life, is not from the Father, but is from the world." (1 John 2:16)

First, let's talk about the lust of the flesh. Lust is an intense desire or appetite, usually associated with sexual desires. God knows we have physical desires, and these desires left unchecked can lead us into some dark places. Eve was obsessed with the forbidden fruit, and more importantly with the lie of the devil, who told her, "If you eat this, you will be just like God." Sinful lust occurs as an overpowering desire that you must struggle to resist, even though you know that God has forbidden it.

Next, John mentions the "Lust of the Eyes." This is simply the desire to possess what we do not have because of its intense visual appeal. Understand that not all desires are sinful. Consider food, for instance. We all have to eat to survive, and one of life's greatest pleasures is sitting down to a meal of our favorite food. It is not only the taste of the food that appeals to us, but its aroma, and the way it looks. Consider, for instance, a Thanksgiving table, set with fine china and your best silverware—with a beautiful turkey on a platter in the center of the table, surrounded by steaming bowls of stuffing, mashed potatoes and gravy, green beans, cranberry sauce and yeasty rolls. It is, a presentation that makes the mouth water and impacts all the senses.

Again, there is nothing wrong with having a meal like this once in a while. But if it becomes an obsession, and enjoyment of good food turns into lust and gluttony, then we have perverted something good and turned it into something sinful.

The same thing is true of sex. God made sex, and like everything else He created, it is very good. (See Genesis 1:31.) But sex is meant to be shared by one man and one woman who love each other and have pledged their lives to one other. Men, in particular, are sexually stimulated by what they see. Therefore, we must be careful about what we look at. We are not to turn our eyes loose on any beautiful woman who comes into our view. As Jesus said, "I tell you that anyone who looks upon a woman lustfully has already committed adultery with her in his heart." (Matthew 5:28)

When it is channeled correctly, sex is a beautiful thing, and a means of propagating the human race. But when it is allowed to rage out of control it leads to promiscuity, adultery, rape, homosexuality, beastiality, pedophilia and many other perversions. What is designed as a loving act becomes something harmful and cruel.

You may recall how Satan used the lust of the eyes to tempt Eve in the Garden of Eden. Eve looked at the forbidden fruit and saw that it was pleasing to the eye. (Genesis 3:6)

Do you remember the old Children's song, "I Washed My Hands this Morning"? J.H. Rosecrans wrote the song for little boys and girls to hear, but the lessons it teaches are useful at any age:

"I washed my hands this morning
O very clean and white
And lent them both to Jesus
To work for Him till night

"Little feet, be careful
Where you take me to
Anything for Jesus
Only let me do

"I told my ears to listen

Quite closely all day through
For any act of kindness
Such little hands can do

"My eyes are set to watch them
About their work or play
To keep them out of mischief
For Jesus' sake all day."

Finally, John talks about the Pride of Life. This term refers to arrogance, boastfulness or similar behavior that comes from the love of this world. The Pride of Life is yet another trick Satan used on Eve in the Garden of Eden. She saw that the forbidden fruit was appealing to her appetite (Lust of the Flesh), appealing to the eye, (Lust of the Eyes) and perhaps most tempting of all, if she ate it, she would become like God (the Pride of Life).

Satan is still using tricks like these today to try to lead us into sin. If you have any doubts about this, just turn on your television, watch a movie or scan the magazine covers at your local newsstand. You will see plenty of sexual come-ons and other messages that are designed to appeal to greed and covetousness. Perhaps you've seen the bumper sticker that says, "He who dies with the most toys wins." Funny, in a way, but yet terribly sad. The race to see who can accumulate the most things can never be won. In fact, it is a race you don't even want to enter.

God does not want you to conform to this world. He wants you to renew your mind, to be transformed. (Romans 12:2) Turn over to Matthew 7:13, and you will read, "Enter through the narrow gate. For wide is the gate and broad is the road that leads to destruction, and many enter through it."

In order to stay on the narrow road, you must learn to say no to the temptations of the flesh, whether they come to you in the form of food, sex, drugs, money or any other "worldly" fashion. The more you say "no," the easier it becomes. You might even want to practice saying, "No, I won't betray God to chase after the things of the world."

The book of James tells us that if we resist the devil, He will flee from us. Conversely, when we draw near to the Lord, he will draw near to us. (James 4:7-8) We must learn to resist Satan, no matter how many times he may attack. As Paul tells us in the book of Ephesians:

> *"Put on the full armor of God, so that you can take your stand against the devil's schemes. For our struggle is not against flesh and blood, but against the rulers, against the authorities, against the powers of this dark world and against the spiritual forces of evil in the Heavenly realms. Therefore put on the full armor of God, so that when the day of evil comes, you may be able to stand your ground, and after you have done everything, to stand. Stand firm then, with the belt of truth buckled around your waist, with the breastplate of righteousness in place, and with your feet fitted with the*

readiness that comes from the gospel of peace. In addition to all this, take up the shield of faith, with which you can extinguish all the flaming arrows of the evil one. Take the helmet of salvation and the sword of the Spirit, which is the word of God."

In Hosea 4:1, the Bible says: *"Hear the word of the Lord, you Israelites, because the L*ORD *has a charge to bring against you who live in the land: 'There is no faithfulness, no love, no acknowledgment of God in the land...'*

In other words, it's not being a good Catholic or saying the sinner's prayer that gets you to Heaven. It's getting to know your Lord and having a personal relationship with Christ. When you know God for who He is, and what Holy means to Him, it will affect every aspect of your life. The more you know about your Savior the more wisdom you will have. *"For the Lord gives wisdom; from His mouth come knowledge and understanding."* (Proverbs 2:6) Go on over to the ninth chapter, verse ten, and you'll find, *"The fear of the Lord is the beginning of wisdom, And the Knowledge of the Holy One is understanding."*

When God knows you want a closer relationship with Him, He will open your eyes.

If you haven't already done so, I urge you to start reading about Jesus in the first four books of the New Testament – Matthew, Mark, Luke and John. As you learn about Him, your life will be transformed and you'll find yourself thinking, "I wish I had known this a long time ago." Your understanding of what is going on in the world will begin to make sense. The impact on your family and friends will be astonishing. You will discover that love is not just a word, but a Person.

You would not be reading this book if God had not intended it – so please let Him speak to you through my words, even though I know they are inadequate to reveal His majesty, power, grace and love. He cares deeply about you and wants you to understand His ways, not man's ways. Let Him open your eyes, let Him share His heart with you.

CHAPTER ELEVEN

SO WHICH IS IT: SALVATION BY WORKS OR SALVATION BY GRACE?

F rom personal experience, I can attest that Catholicism is based primarily on ceremony and ritual. I suggest that it is a religion of bondage filled with do's and don'ts compared to the simple message of the Gospel of Jesus Christ. While Catholics espouse a "catechism," the oral teaching of religious doctrine typically in the form of questions and answers, the true words of salvation are rarely taught. I've found that Catholics—including priests—most often reply "I think so" or "I hope so" when asked if they're going to Heaven.

I pray that all who read this understand that God wants us to know without a doubt if we are going to Heaven. God is not a gameplayer, and He makes the "rules" clear. We are His children, and we are on earth to do His will and to win others to Christ through sharing the Gospel and through our example as living lights to the world.

What do the words "Are you saved" mean? As it is primarily thought to be a Protestant term, the phrase can be an immediate turn off to Catholics. Most have not been taught—and therefore do not understand—salvation by grace. Having been instructed that salvation is dependent on works, including the recitation of prayers for forgiveness, the idea that we are to rest in the magnificent work God did through Christ is unsettling. The truth that we can do nothing to merit salvation is too simple to believe. Surely, we must do something to earn so great a gift! But the key word is "gift." A gift is given freely. We don't earn gifts or pay for gifts. Doing so negates the word itself.

Ephesians 2:8-9 tells us, *"For it is by grace you have been saved, through faith—and this is not from yourselves, it is the gift of God—not by works, so that no one can boast."*

We cannot, by works or any other deed, do anything to merit the salvation Christ has obtained for us. Clearly, the only thing we can do in response is say, *"Thanks be to God for His indescribable gift!"* (2 Corinthians 9:15).

We cannot add anything to what God orchestrated. God created us all; He loves us all; He wants to save us all. We need only accept His offer of salvation through Christ's sacrifice. Sadly, it is often our pride that rejects the simplicity of the Gospel.

Let's go back to the cross for a few minutes. God never acts arbitrarily. His works are ordered and driven by His supernatural wisdom.

Isaiah 53:12 tells us:

"...He poured out his life unto death,

and was numbered with the transgressors.

For he bore the sin of many, and

made intercession for the transgressors."

Christ would be "*numbered with the transgressors*" (the two thieves), which added to the shame of being hung naked on a tree. In addition to this physical humiliation, Christ took upon Himself the worst of everything—the sin, sicknesses, and diseases of the world—and in so doing fulfilled Isaiah's prophecy.

God decreed in His infinite wisdom that the Creator of the universe be born among the lowly and the beasts of the field. After His three-year ministry, He was tried illegally, scourged to the point where He no longer looked like a human, and then hung on the cross to die a horrible death. All of this came to pass in accordance with God's plan and by His hand and counsel as He willed it should be done. *(See Acts 4:28.)*

As we have seen, on the cross, one of the thieves ridiculed Jesus. The other turned to the Messiah. "*Then he said, 'Remember me when you come into your kingdom.' Jesus answered him, 'Truly I tell you, today you will be with me in paradise'*". (Luke 23:42-43)

If works are a prerequisite for salvation, what could this criminal possible do to earn entrance into Heaven? Absolutely nothing. While he had a change of heart, he was already doomed to die, most likely within hours. If redemption were something to be earned, he had no time left on this earth to perform good deeds, participate in rituals, or recite litanies. How was it that Jesus could say to him, "Today you will be with Me in paradise"? Because the thief simply trusted in Christ and believed in who He was. Just like us, he could only offer his sin and shame to Jesus and receive salvation in exchange.

Even Mary, the mother of Jesus, prayed in what is known as the Magnificat, *"And my spirit rejoices in God my Savior"* (Luke 1:47). By calling God her Savior, she acknowledged her own sinful state. People who are without sin do not need a Savior. Romans 3:23-24 reinforces this, saying, *"for all have sinned and fall short of the glory of God, and all are justified freely by his grace through the redemption that came by Christ Jesus."* All have sinned. No exceptions.

Thank God for His all-sufficient grace! Without it, we would all— and, again, all—no exceptions—be destined for life here and hereafter without Him. Grace is unmerited. It is God's goodness toward those who have neither claim nor reason to expect His divine favor.

Let's take a look at a young man born and raised a Catholic, who loved the Lord and who greatly loved the Blessed Mother. I was that young man! I never believed I was good enough to pray to the Lord. I felt closer to Mary because she was a mother and surely understood young aggressive boys. I found it easier to pray to her. For years, I uttered this prayer every night: "O most beautiful flower of Mount Carmel, fruitful vine, splendor of Heaven, blessed mother of the Son of God, immaculate virgin, assist me in this my necessity."

Then I came across Matthew 6:6-9 where Jesus says, *"But when you pray, go into your room, close the door and pray to your Father, who is unseen. Then your Father, who sees what is done in secret, will reward you. And when you pray, do not keep on babbling like pagans, for they think they will be heard because of their many words. Do not be like them, for your Father knows what you need before you ask him. This, then, is how you should pray: Our Father in Heaven, hallowed be your name..."*

Jesus made it clear that we are to pray only to the Father in His name. It therefore follows that, if we are to pray *only* to the Father, we are not to pray to saints, Mary, or anyone else. The Apostle Paul reinforces how we are to pray in Philippians 4:6: *"Do not be anxious about anything, but in every situation, by prayer and petition, with thanksgiving, present your requests to God."* To God. Not to Mary. Not to saints.

I was convicted by the Living Word and, from that point on, prayed directly—and only—to God.

In the Old Testament, prayers, offerings, and sacrifices were administered through the priests (of the Levitical order) who stood as mediators between God and man. Only these priests were allowed into the Holy of Holies in the temple to intervene on behalf of the people through blood sacrifices. But Christ, as our ultimate and final High Priest, the Lamb of God Himself, shattered the wall between God and man. After Christ ascended into Heaven following His resurrection, man no longer needed an intermediary other than Jesus. We could now go directly to God through Jesus alone.

Jesus Himself proclaimed in John 14:6, *"I am the way and the truth and the life. No one comes to the Father except through me."*

King David was one of God's strongest and most trusted friends. Even though he loved God and had dedicated his life to Him, the Scripture describes David's sin and the outcome. Psalm 32:3-4 tells us that David was weak and miserable when he harbored unconfessed sin.

> *"When I kept silent, my bones wasted away through my groaning all day long. For day and night Your hand was heavy on me; my strength was sapped as in the heat of summer."*

Sin weakens a person oftentimes to the point of sickness. But the Bible gives us the remedy in 1 John 1:9:

"If we confess our sins, he is faithful and just and will forgive us our sins and purify us from all unrighteousness." Confession is part of the sanctification process. Confessing to God enables us to practice humility. James 4:6 tells us, *"But he gives us more grace. That is why Scripture says: 'God opposes the proud but shows favor to the humble.'"*

The Bible is talking here about confession to God, admitting our sins to Him and asking for His forgiveness. The Catholic Church defines confession as "the telling of sins to an authorized priest for the purpose of obtaining forgiveness." According to this premise, an "authorized priest" not only has the power to forgive sins but also has jurisdiction over the persons who come to him. This comes about as part of the Bishop's role, which he confers to his priests.

And yet, there is no mention of auricular confession in the Bible. In addition, there is no mention in church history for the first thousand years! Renowned Christian writers, such as Augustine, Jerome, Origen, etc., never referenced auricular confession. Neither is there any discussion of kneeling before a priest, especially for the airing of an individual's sins. Confession first emerged in the fifth century on a "voluntary basis" edict of Pope Leo the Great.

The book of James does talk about confessing our sins to one another in order that we may be healed. (James 5:16) But nowhere does the Bible tells us to confess to a priest. Obviously, when my behavior has hurt someone, I need to go to them and ask for their forgiveness. It's vital to live in complete honesty and transparency with my brothers and sisters in the Lord, but this is not what the Catholic Church is talking about when it speaks of confession.

During the "Dark Ages," the church held a tremendous amount of political power, with the Catholic Church basically ruling the known world. Priests, through the confessional, gleaned priority information from the laity and passed this information along to church leaders in Rome.

In this period, the church had the power to tax as well as execute laws, and amassed a fortune, which was not taxed. The common belief was that the only way to get to Heaven was through the Catholic

Church. The laity gave a tenth of their earnings to the church, in addition to buying indulgences.

Under Pope Innocent III, following the Fourth Lateran Council (1215 AD), the word "compulsory" was attached to both the confessing of sins to an authorized priest and transubstantiation, or the changing of the communion bread and wine into the literal body and blood of Christ. We see the beginnings of papal and priestly power with these two doctrines.

As a young man, my friends and I frequented bars and pool halls and, on many occasions, found a few spirited lady friends. Being Catholic, I went to church on Saturday afternoon for confession. I'll admit I didn't go every week, but I made it there at least once every three months.

After confession, I would recite the required penance—usually a "5&5" — which means five Hail Marys and five Our Fathers, or whatever I was instructed by the priest. But time after time, after I slipped into bad behavior, I asked myself, "What happened to the Holy Spirit? Did He jump out prior to my slipping up or what?" I came to understand that the Holy Spirit is grieved when we sin, but He does not leave us. *"And do not grieve the Holy Spirit of God, with whom you were sealed for the day of redemption."* (Ephesians 4:30 Thank the Lord for the word "sealed"!

Looking again at David, the Scriptures are clear that he was not a perfect man. He lied, murdered, and committed adultery. But David was still a man after God's own heart. Though we do not lose our standing as saved when we sin, fellowship with the Father is broken because of that sin as long as it remains unconfessed. The cure is repentance. God is merciful and will restore us to full fellowship with Him when we repent – which means to turn away from our sins – to literally turn our backs on them and walk away from them.

If we delay in our response to the conviction of the Holy Spirit tugging on our hearts, we suffer. Our sin will constantly be on our minds. We often find ourselves depressed and downhearted until we confess our sin to God and ask for His forgiveness.

While living in unforgiveness can seriously affect our body's health, it also negatively impacts our testimony to the world and our credibility when declaring the Good News.

As we have discussed previously, the Roman Catholic Church divides sin into classes. Venial sins lead to purgatory but are considered small and pardonable offenses against God that are easily reconciled by good works. Mortal sins, on the other hand, are extremely serious.

Be assured that the Bible makes no distinction between sins. Sin is sin. In God's eyes all sins are "mortal."

Ezekiel 18:20 says, *"The one who sins is the one who will die. The child will not share the guilt of the parent, nor will the parent share the guilt of the child. The righteousness of the righteous will be credited to them, and the wickedness of the wicked will be charged against them."*

And the Apostle Paul teaches us in the New Testament *"For the wages of sin is death, but the gift of God is eternal life in Christ Jesus our Lord."* (Romans 6:23)

The Scripture is clear in James 2:10: *"For whoever keeps the whole law and yet stumbles at just one point is guilty of breaking all of it."*

The distinction between mortal and venial is non-existent. Sin to God is sin and punishable by death. Distinguishing between venial and mortal sin is an attempt to mitigate the seriousness of all sin and lessen the severity of disobeying God.

Through studying the Word of God, I came to understand that a priest cannot forgive sins. *Only God can.* "Who can forgive sins but God alone?" *(Mark 2:7b)* Are you troubled by the wrong things you have done in your life? Are you carrying around a heavy load of guilt everywhere you go? Take your burden of sin to God. Ask Him to take it away, and He will. Listen to what the Bible says:

"The LORD is compassionate and merciful,
slow to get angry and filled with unfailing love.
He will not constantly accuse us,
nor remain angry forever.
He does not punish us for all our sins;
he does not deal harshly with us, as we deserve.
For his unfailing love toward those who fear him
is as great as the height of the Heavens above the earth.
He has removed our sins as far from us as the east is from
the west." (Psalm 103:8-12)

Chapter Twelve

Where will you Spend Eternity?

H*ave you spent much time thinking about the life that lies beyond this one? King David did:*

> *"Show me, Lord, my life's end*
> *and the number of my days;*
> *let me know how fleeting my life is.*
> *You have made my days a mere handbreadth;*
> *the span of my years is as nothing before you.*
> *Everyone is but a breath,*
> *even those who seem secure." (*Psalm 39:4-5)

David exposed his very soul in this Psalm. His words are a far cry from the advice he gave in Psalm 37:7, where he said to *"rest in the Lord"* (NKJ). Psalm 39 was written late in David's life and reflects upon his thinking about death. He experienced frustration and admitted in verse 3 that *"My heart grew hot within me..."* Then he says to the Lord,

"Show me, Lord, my life's end and the number of my days; let me know how fleeting my life is." (verse 4)

Think about what David is saying here. He was a shepherd, a musician, a warrior, and, without a doubt, one of the most famous people of his time. Yet he clearly understood the shortness of life and that man is but a vapor. But he also understood that nothing was more important than God.

David considered humanity in general and the typical lack of interest in the brevity of life. But he also considered life and the consequences of actions. He acknowledged that his hope was in God, not in himself, and he fell on the mercy of the Lord. David prayed for relief from his affliction. His prayers turned to tears in his desperation.

We all must choose.

"See, I set before you today life and prosperity, death and destruction. For I command you today to love the Lord your God, to walk in obedience to him, and to keep his commands, decrees, and laws; then you will live and increase, and the Lord your God will bless you in the land you are entering to possess.

But if your heart turns away and you are not obedient, and if you are drawn away to bow down to other gods and worship them, I declare to you this day that you will certainly be destroyed. You will not live long in the land you are crossing the Jordan to enter and possess.

This day I call the Heavens and the earth as witnesses against you that I have set before you life and death, blessings and curses. Now choose life, so that you and your children may live and that you may love the Lord your God, listen to his voice, and hold fast to him. For the Lord is your life, and he will give you many years in the land he swore to give to your fathers, Abraham, Isaac and Jacob."
(Deuteronomy 30:15-20)

The early Christian Church was persecuted, with thousands of innocent men, women and even children martyred for their faith. Christians refused to participate in pagan rituals and celebrations and were consequently blackballed from holding public office.

Keep this in mind as I explain why this book is important to Catholics and their spiritual growth. Catholics may ask if believing in purgatory will keep them out of Heaven, if wearing a scapular is a bad thing, or if praying the rosary is a good thing to do. Devout Catholics who are reading this are undoubtedly defending and making a case for why they should continue to do these things.

But obedience and disobedience are the real issues. If obedience is the acceptance of God's authority, then disobedience is rebellion and distrust of God. Disobedience is a belief in the same lie that tricked

Adam and Even in the Garden of Eden. It says, "I will be as God," and lives life yielding to self-will. Who we obey is critical to our spiritual health.

Will you know who Christ is when you get to Heaven? If, while you roamed the earth, you traveled with your best friend, Jesus, you will recognize Him immediately. If, on the other hand, you only knew of Him, the outcome will be different. Saying you believe in Christ and realizing your understanding never traveled from your mind to your heart is the real salvation issue.

Micah 6:8 tells us, *"He has shown you, O mortal, what is good. And what does the Lord require of you? To act justly and to love mercy and to walk humbly with your God."*

Obedience is critical to pleasing God. Deuteronomy 11:26-28 basically tells us that we will be blessed if we obey and cursed if we disobey.

Thousands of years of disobedience have taken a terrible toll on this planet of hours. Wars too numerous to count, millions of failed marriages, deadly crime eating at the hearts and souls in our cities, the development of horrible weapons of mass destruction, diseases that have killed millions, plagues, terrorist slaughters of innocent people, the list goes on and on.

No one living a life filled with disobedient acts can claim assurance that Heaven is in their future. There is a solution. A solution God provided in Jesus Christ, the Messiah, promised to man in the Garden of Eden.

What exactly is God looking for in man? God looks at the heart. He wants us to obey and trust Him even when we do not understand. God, all-powerful and all-knowing, works all things to fulfill His purposes. Psalm 57:2 (NLT) says, *"I cry out to God Most High, to God who will fulfill his purpose for me."*

God is in control. We understand that God hates certain things, and it is obviously best to avoid them.

Proverbs 6:16-19 tells us,

> *"There are six things the Lord hates, seven that are detestable to him:*
> *haughty eyes,*
> *a lying tongue,*
> *hands that shed innocent blood,*
> *a heart that devises wicked schemes,*
> *feet that are quick to rush into evil,*
> *a false witness who pours out lies*
> *and a person who stirs up conflict in the community."*

God's compassion and love for man moves Him to hate sin. Let's look closer at Proverbs 6:16-19.

God hates a proud look. Pride caused Lucifer the archangel to rebel and fall from Heaven. Pride keeps many from accepting the Lord.

The Bible makes it clear. *"Pride goes before destruction, a haughty spirit before a fall."* (Proverbs 16:18)

The Lord hates a lying tongue. A child doesn't need to be taught to lie. Sadly, it's instinctive. A lying tongue brings about so many other sins—slander, embezzlement, libel, not keeping one's word, deceit, the ruin of reputations, and more.

Hands that shed innocent blood. While we may be convinced we would never commit murder, Jesus redefines the word from God's perspective by saying that anyone who hates his brother has committed murder in his heart. 1 John 3:15 reaffirms this, saying, *"Anyone who hates a brother or sister is a murderer, and you know that no murderer has eternal life residing in him."* It's sobering to think that, in God's eyes, we murder by hating. I don't believe anyone can claim to have never hated someone. We are all, therefore, guilty of murder.

Next is **the heart that devises evil schemes.** Harboring sinful intentions is sin. Just looking at a woman with lustful eyes is the equivalent of committing adultery. (Matthew 5:28)

God hates feet that are quick to run after evil. People flagrantly violate God's laws and actually boast about their mischief.

Finally, God hates a false witness who pours out lies and stirs up discontent. Slander. Lies. Gossip. All of these stem from an unbridled tongue. We are admonished in Ephesians 4:31 to *"Get rid of all bitterness, rage and anger, brawling and slander, along with every form of malice."*

Our relationship with our God is like that between a parent and child. As our parent, God loves all of us. On many occasions Jesus referred to God as His Father. Since we cannot see God with our physical eyes, our relationship with Him is developed and grows by faith. This relationship continues to grow the more time we spend in His Word.

God loves us more than we can imagine. *"Are not five sparrows sold for two pennies? Yet not one of them is forgotten by God. Indeed, the very hairs of your head are all numbered. Don't be afraid; you are worth more than many sparrows."* (Luke 12:6-7).

We cannot say that God loves us because we loved Him first. The exact opposite is true. 1 John 4:19 clearly tells us that we love Him because He first loved us. God not only gives love, He *is* love!

Throughout this book, we've talking the Roman Catholic Church. My desire, in all of this, is to help people who have become tangled up in Catholic dogma so much that they have missed the grace of God. This error is not unique to Catholicism. Human beings tend to worship the gifts God gives us instead of keeping our eyes on God Himself.

I think of what happened in the Methodist Church, which grew out of the teachings of John and Charles Wesley.

Their purpose was to provide structure, and they set forth rules—or "methods"—for the congregation to follow, assuring them of spending eternity in Heaven. Over time people began looking to the method rather than to Jesus as the way to get to Heaven. This actually equates to relying on works for our salvation.

Following any set rules or particular method does not guarantee anyone Heaven. Trust in Jesus is what is required of us all. We can either choose the world or we step out in faith and choose Heaven and God's plan of salvation.

"Now faith is confidence in what we hope for and assurance about what we do not see... And without faith it is impossible to please God, because anyone who comes to him must believe that he exists and that he rewards those who earnestly seek him." (Hebrews 11:1, 6)

Now is the time to search your heart. Now is the time to honestly confess what you believe. Do you say in your heart, "I'm a good person and deserve to go to Heaven." Or perhaps, "I go to mass and communion every Sunday, and I expect to go to Heaven because of my devotion." Or even, "I don't steal or lie, surely God will allow me into Heaven."

Can you say without a doubt that you are going to Heaven? God knows the answer. He will not be duped.

"And you, my son Solomon, acknowledge the God of your father, and serve him with wholehearted devotion and with a willing mind, for the Lord searches every heart and understands every desire and every thought. If you seek him, he will be found by you; but if you forsake him, he will reject you forever. (1 Chronicles 28:9)

God is willing to be found. *"You will seek Me and find Me when you seek me with all your heart."* (*Jeremiah 29:13*).

The question is a simple one:

Are you searching with all your heart?

God wants us all to understand the story of redemption. It's not about joining a specific religious denomination. It's about fellowship-ping with other believers in a church that depends on Christ. It's about sharing the Good News with the lost. Our entire existence is based on glorifying God, trusting God, and depending on God in all things.

God is in charge. He sits on the throne of the universe. Through Jesus, He provided a way for man to avoid the consequences of sin. The blood of Jesus provides forgiveness for our sins. Our response to God's love must be thankfulness and complete surrender.

May God bless you and keep you, now, and for all eternity.